MINGMING II

& the Islands of the Ice

ROGER D. TAYLOR

MINGMING II

& the Islands of the Ice

*With illustrations
from the author's log-book*

F

THE FITZROY PRESS

Published by The FitzRoy Press 2016.

𝓕
The FitzRoy Press
5 Regent Gate
Waltham Cross
Herts EN8 7AF

ISBN 978 0955803 574

A catalogue record for this book is available from the British Library

Publishing management by Troubador Publishing Ltd, Leicester, UK
Printed and bound in the UK by TJ International, Padstow, Cornwall

MIX
Paper from
responsible sources
FSC   FSC® C013056
www.fsc.org

'*On peut tout détruire en voulant aller plus vite que la nature…*'
Bernard Moitessier, *La Longue Route.*

(*'One can destroy everything by trying to outpace nature…*'
Bernard Moitessier, *The Long Way)*

Contents

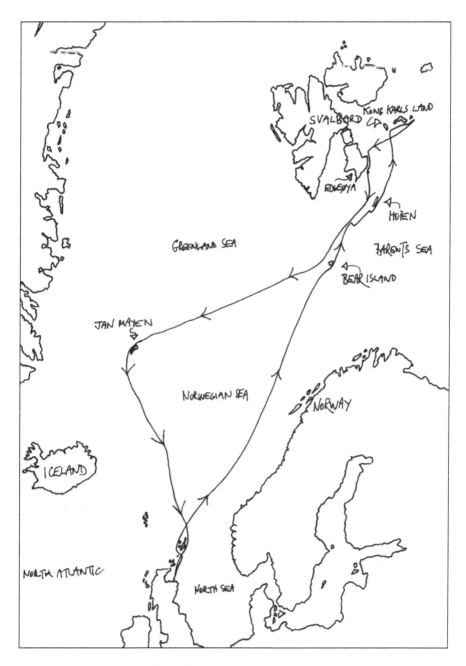

Mingming II's *2014 Voyage*

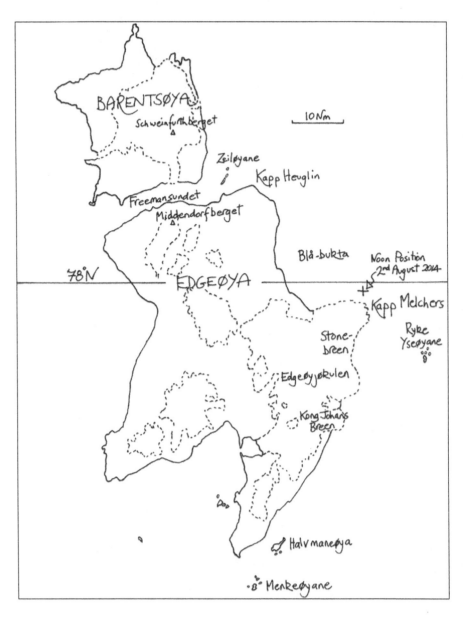

Barentsøya and Edgeøya, north-east Svalbard

The following labels appear on the map:

BARENTSØYA

Schweinfurthberget △

Zeiløyane

Kapp Heuglin

10 Nm

Freemansundet

Middendorfberget △

Blå-bukta

Noon Position
2nd August 2014

78°N

EDGEØYA

Kapp Melchers

Stone-breen

Ryke
Yseøyane

Edgeøyjøkulen

Kong Johans
Breen

Halvmaneøya

Menkeøyane

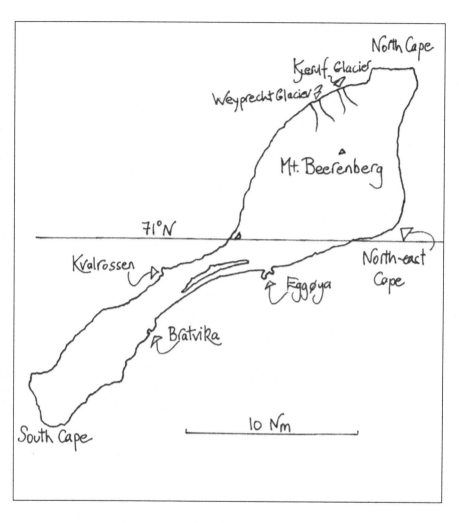

Jan Mayen

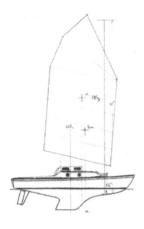

1

We had sailed twenty thousand miles in northern seas and now *Mingming* was tired. Her mainsail was a patchwork; her mast, thirty years old, was scored with the stigmata of storm and calm. Heading back home from 80°North in 2011, I began to feel that I had asked enough of her. Lightly built and always willing, she had skipped her way across everything the ocean could throw at her. She had been a marvellous companion, but now needed either rest or a total re-fit.

Something else was gnawing away at me: the need to create another boat. It was nearly forty years since I had built my first little ocean cruiser *Roc*, but the compulsion was still there. What better adventure is there for a man than to hammer together a tiny craft and to sail it across the wide world? The idea still burned as strongly as it did in my boyhood. Now, though, it was overlaid with the guile of age and with the knowledge hard-won from many thousands of hours at sea.

Mingming had taught me a lot, and my head was swimming with ideas for an improved version. I felt that I had one more boat in me. The challenge was irresistible: to create the ideal small and simple ocean cruiser; my final word on the matter.

My drawing pads were, as ever, filled with preliminary sketches and plans. For a while I considered building a complete boat from scratch. It would take too long, though. I wanted to be sailing rather than boat-building. In a world over-laden with unused and neglected yachts, it seemed impertinent to be adding yet another hull to the pile. It would be quicker and less wasteful to find an old and unloved yacht, to strip it down to the bare hull and deck, and to rebuild it to my own specifications.

For half a year I drove around the country looking at older yachts in obscure coastal corners, examining the detritus of a thousand dreams. Gradually the choices narrowed until I knew exactly what I wanted: a triple-keeled Achilles 24. This was the design that came closest to a slightly scaled-up Corribee; a bigger and more robust *Mingming*. Fine-lined and with low freeboard, it was designed by Oliver Lee of Burnham-on-Crouch, and was therefore related to the redoubtable Squib racing keelboat. I talked to many past and present Achilles owners; every one of them praised its sailing abilities. About six hundred were built, and well built too. Chris Butler, who produced the yachts in his South Wales factory, had won his class in the Observer Singlehanded Transatlantic Race. As the starting point for creating *Mingming II*, the Achilles seemed ideal.

I found the one I wanted tucked away in a broker's yard in Neyland, South Wales. At first glance it was in a disastrous state, with its rotting rubbing strake, bilges full of water, filthy and chaotic interior, worn-out fittings and corroded electrics. The hull and deck were sound, though, and that was all that mattered. Given that I was going to tear the boat apart, there was no point paying for a smart interior or fancy gadgetry.

By February 2012 I had the new boat back at my base at Rice and Cole's yard at Burnham-on-Crouch, lined up alongside *Mingming*. Although she was just three feet longer overall – 23' 9" as opposed to *Mingming's* 20' 9" – she seemed enormous by comparison. At this stage too there was little to suggest sisterly likeness, apart from some similarity in their lines. Over the next two years that was to change.

I quickly sold on *Mingming II's* Bermudan rig: mast, rigging and sails. One of the central tasks of the rebuild was to convert her to a junk rig. I had long since concluded that this was by far the easiest and most versatile rig for small-boat singlehanded sailing. This was, too, one of the principal areas where I felt I could make huge improvements.

With the mast gone and the decks cleared I set to work.

The rebuild took nearly two and a half years to complete, working at weekends and for three months full-time during two summers. The boat was transformed inside and out, following the principles I had developed over many years. The central keel was removed and re-bedded, and the thirty year-old studs replaced. Every single deck fitting was taken off and every resultant hole plugged. The few fittings I retained were re-bedded. Every skin fitting was removed and its holes sealed. Foam-filled compartments were created fore and aft behind watertight bulkheads. An immensely strong mast step was built forward to take the new mast. I strengthened the foredeck and built a massive flange and partners for the mast to pass through. The forward hatch area was remodelled to take a proper watertight hatch. The long and unsightly acrylic windows were replaced with strong plywood cabin-sides and small portholes, identical in diameter to those of *Mingming*.

The main structural changes were made at the after end of the cabin. There I first built a raised dog-house. This was designed to give me an area of full standing headroom, but more importantly to give me full all-round vision from inside the boat. I called it my observation pod. The central hatch was fitted in its roof. Much of the after end of the cabin and the forward part of the cockpit was then cut out, enabling me to extend the cabin aft. This gave me more room inside, better access to the aft internal stowage areas, and reduced the size of the cockpit. The main working hatch was built into this section, along with its protective side coamings and folding spray hood.

I sealed the cockpit locker lids with fibreglass, so that *Mingming II* was by then totally watertight above and below the waterline. A new rudder was built and the stainless steel rudder tube replaced with solid stainless steel bar. I made a longer and more robust tiller that could be reached easily from the working hatch.

As the work progressed *Mingming II's* livery was gradually changed. I painted her topsides black and finished off the decks and cabin in Mingming Grey. By now she was starting to look the part.

It is a necessary rite of passage for every yacht I own to scrape off, by hand, every inch of anti-fouling, bringing the hull below the waterline back to the gelcoat, or to bare wood. It is a long and in many ways soulless task, but it serves several useful purposes. It forces you to examine the hull and to familiarise yourself with every subtlety of its curvature. It helps you develop strong shoulder muscles and infinite patience. There is something satisfying, too, about starting a-fresh with a clean and smooth hull.

I bought a municipal lamp post. This was a magnificent tapered aluminium tube forty-five feet long. I cut off the bottom sixteen feet to give me exactly what I wanted: a robust mast twenty-nine feet long, eight inches in diameter at the base and three inches at the top. I painted it with nine coats of epoxy paint and added a stainless steel masthead fitting welded up by a local agricultural engineer.

I needed a particularly strong mast because I had designed and made what some may consider an over-size sail. This was to cope with the extremely light winds typical of the high Arctic in summer. In any case, the junk rig is so easily reefed that it seemed better to have too much sail rather than too little.

I sewed the sail on the dining room table during the week after Christmas 2012. It was constructed of seven panels. The top four panels were joined as per a normal sail, but the bottom three panels were all separate entities. The sail was therefore in four parts. This was for several reasons. Firstly the sewing machine and space I had could not have coped with an entire sail. Secondly I liked the idea of having some separate panels that could be taken off and repaired easily, or even interchanged.

The principal reason, though, was to do with the design of the sail. Whereas *Mingming's* sail was cut completely flat, in the traditional junk style, I wanted to try out the more powerful modern system of cambered panels. There are various ways that this camber can be achieved. For the top four panels I used the normal sail-makers' method of broad-seaming: joining pieces of cloth already cut to the appropriate curves. For the bottom three individual panels I invented a system that uses cloth hinges to attach the flat panel to the sail battens. The aerodynamic curve is built into the hinge system.

The sail was so crazy that I felt it deserved an appropriate title. I christened it the Triple H sail: the horizontally hinged hybrid. From an aesthetic and engineering point of view, the proper number of panels was probably six. I began to view the additional seventh panel as the sail's turbo-charger for very light airs, giving rise eventually to the sail's full title: the Triple H TB.

I built the yard and boom from ordinary 'yellow' pine

from the local DIY store, laminated for strength and stability. In fact throughout the rebuild I used either recycled timber and plywood, or else standard quality lumber and ply. I was very careful, though, to epoxy all end grains, and where possible to give a protective coat of fibreglass.

By the end of the summer of 2013 most of the main structural work was complete. The interior was by no means finished, but I decided that it was time to go sailing. I needed to try out the new rig. In particular I wanted to see how it balanced. I wanted too to get an idea of how all the changes had affected the trim of the boat. I still had to make decisions about how I would distribute the heavy stowage – food, water, anchors and so on – and felt that some sailing trials would help me in this.

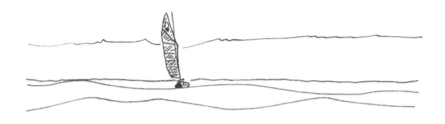

2

On a wet September Monday *Mingming II*, on her trailer, was hitched to the yard tractor and pulled the short distance to the launching crane. The slings were attached and within a few minutes she was raised high in the air to be swung out over the Burnham-on-Crouch sea wall and into the water. As she moved slowly seawards forty feet in the air I could really appreciate, for the first time, the sweetness of her lines.

I was, of course, a little apprehensive. How would she float? Would she be down by the nose? Her keels kissed the water then disappeared. The slings started to slacken, dropped further and there she was, floating free and as sweetly as a swan. Michael, the yard foreman, and not a man to be easily impressed, let out a loud '*Don't she float nice!*'. She certainly did, almost perfectly trimmed and sitting light and easily in the water. It was a moment of some relief, and I knew there and then that she was going to be a good'un.

For the best part of two months I sailed her on the River

Crouch and had the most tremendous fun. For a start it was a welcome change to be away from sawdust and epoxy and sore knees. It was a delight to feel *Mingming II* come alive for the first time. More than anything, though, I had a riotous time because she sailed so absurdly well.

The junk rig is a supple and supremely practical rig. With the wind free it is very powerful; to windward it can sometimes struggle. Many junk rigs have been put on yachts with indifferent sailing qualities, very often using less efficient split rigs for ease of handling, and very often using conservative sail areas. The sailors of Bermudan-rigged yachts have no expectation, as a result, that their performance is ever going to be challenged by that of a junk.

It was a joy, then, to be at the helm of an inherently fast yacht with a huge and powerful rig. As *Mingming II* was largely unfinished inside she was very light too, to the point of tenderness. This did not bother me at all. I knew that once she was in full cruising trim she would stiffen up.

I was pleased too that it took very little adjustment to get *Mingming II's* sail more or less crease-free and performing as well as I ever could have hoped. On *Mingming* I had introduced headsails to help windward performance, particularly in light airs, and I was now glad to be rid of them. With just one sail for all conditions, handling the yacht was simple and easy. *Mingming II* had no engine, of course, but leaving and picking up her mooring was generally straightforward. I still had to careful, though: the ebb tide could sweep through at three knots or more.

In a normal breeze *Mingming II* could just about hold her own to windward with comparable Bermudan-rigged yachts. She had good speed, although not the extreme pointing ability of many modern Bermudan yachts. With the wind free she was anybody's match.

Where she really excelled, though, was in light airs. With

so much sail area high on the rig, she could keep tracking smoothly in the faintest of breezes. In these conditions she regularly outpaced yachts considerably bigger. I remained outwardly impassive as we overtook shiny king-sized monsters here and there, causing looks of surprise, puzzlement and sometimes dismay. Inside, though, I glowed with the most appalling smugness.

In general I am not much concerned about speed; there are many more important factors that contribute to making a good ocean cruiser. *Mingming II's* rig had been designed, though, to perform well in calm weather. That, too, was the main reason for choosing a yacht with a longer waterline than her predecessor. I had sewn the sail myself. Perhaps I was entitled to the occasional self-congratulatory moment.

The sailing trials firmed up my ideas about how I would finish off *Mingming II's* interior, and at the end of October she was craned out for the final six months of boatbuilding.

The installation of watertight compartments at the bow meant that, as on *Mingming*, the forward V-berths had been reduced to stowage space only. This area was divided from the main cabin by half bulkheads port and starboard. Aft of this to starboard was the main berth. To port was the compact galley, nothing more than an Origo single burner alcohol stove, as on *Mingming*. Below the stove was an un-insulated locker that served as the boat's fridge. Above it was the chart table that hinged upwards when the stove was in use. Aft of the galley and chart table was the port berth. Having berths to port and starboard was perhaps the main difference inside between *Mingming II* and *Mingming*. It gave what was already a considerably bigger cabin an even more spacious feel, and it would, of course, transform life at sea. I bought foam and material, and with some help from Brenda made the bunk cushions at home.

The whole of the hull and the coach roof was insulated

with one-inch Plastazote foam covered with carpet. The observation pod had been built from massive timbers and thick layers of laminated ply, and I suspected that it would not need insulation, so I left it bare.

I installed the only electrical circuit on board, connecting the solar panel to the battery, switches and LED navigation lights. The huge bilge pump that I had bought new from a friend was installed under the bottom step of the companionway. I take the view that the smaller the yacht, the bigger the pump you need, on the basis that a much smaller amount of water can do a lot more damage much more quickly than on a big boat. I created lots of strong attachment points for the stowage of food and water canisters. I built a whole series of made-to-measure boxes to serve as shelves here and here, and sewed covers for them to keep the contents in.

The interior was painted out with a darkish grey matte paint. With three hatches acting as skylights, and the observation pod and portholes as well, *Mingming II* was well served inside with natural light. I am not keen on glary, over-bright interiors, so was happy to tone it down with a more sombre colour. The upholstery was all in a deep and relaxing green that contrasted well with the grey.

The final exterior job, the construction of bins and covers for the Jordan series drogue, was completed. These were put on the aft end of each cockpit seat, leaving enough room for me to sit there if required.

By the end of May 2014 the new boat was pretty much ready for sea, and after nearly three years ashore, so was I. It was time for some real sailing.

3

The creation of *Mingming II* had absorbed most of my physical and mental energy, leaving little to spare to think about our first voyage together. It would be to the Arctic, of course, and given that the one relatively close northern sea I had not sailed in was the Barents Sea, it would be to the east of Svalbard. But where exactly?

I pulled out my northern charts and started to examine them. I could see straight away that a voyage to Bjørnøya – Bear Island – would be ideal for a shakedown cruise. Situated halfway between the North Cape of Norway and the South Cape of Spitsbergen, in 74°North, it is an island I had long wanted to visit. It lies just over eleven hundred miles from my departure point at Whitehills on the Moray Firth and so is a similar distance to a Plymouth-Azores run.

I settled on Bjørnøya as my target, until my eye ranged further north. For the first time I began to examine in detail the islands to the east of Spitsbergen, the eastern islands, that is, of the Svalbard group. Just one hundred and eighty miles further on from Bjørnøya, to the north-east, lies the narrow worm of an island called Hopen. My curiosity was aroused. *Why not have a look at that too, seeing as I would be so close?* By continuing on to Hopen we would take ourselves much more unequivocally into the Barents Sea, across the shallow waters of the Spitsbergen Banks.

My finger traced out a trajectory further to the north-east and there, another hundred and fifty or so miles on from Hopen, was not one but a whole group of islands: Kong Karls Land. It was too much to resist. Kong Karls Land! The name alone thundered with northern exoticism. How could I not carry on, if at all possible, to Kong Karls Land?

I studied the group in more detail. From west to east there are three main islands: Svenskøya, Kongsøya and Abeløya. What's more, Abeløya, the most northerly, is bisected by the meridian of 79°North. Now my heart soared. *This is more like it! This something we can really get our teeth into!* A voyage merely to Bjørnøya seemed pale by comparison.

On went my finger, on to the north-east, and there was the end of the earth, the last outpost of Svalbard: Kvitøya – White Island. Kvitøya lives up to its name: it is an island composed of nothing but an ice-cap, a circular glacier which, except for a tiny sliver on its south-west perimeter, completely covers the rock on which it rests. It lies just above 80°North. If we could get that far we would match *Mingming's* most northerly latitude to the west of Spitsbergen in 2011.

I knew well enough, though, that to go that far north to the east of Spitsbergen was a quite different proposition. The sea to the north-east of Svalbard is the last area to be clear of ice during the summer. What's more, it often does not clear until late in August, and occasionally, even now, does not clear at all.

My plan of attack was firming up. I would sail first to Bjørnøya, then carry on as far as was feasible to the north-east, exploring the islands as we went. If the sea was clear of ice I might even have a go at sailing right round the north of Svalbard; if not, I would turn back to the south-west and have a look at the bigger islands of eastern Svalbard: Barentsøya and Edgeøya.

There was one more important factor that would have to be decided sooner or later: the route home. I could, of course, simple follow my outward track, returning in a straight line more or less due south. There were two reasons, though, why this did not appeal to me. Firstly it gave the overall voyage an unattractive shape: too much of a direct there-and-back feel. Secondly it did not use the anti-clockwise currents of the Norwegian and Greenland Seas to best advantage. I would be sailing home directly into the North Atlantic Current and losing up to twenty-four miles a day as a result. It would be much more seamanlike to head out to the west and try to pick up the colder south-going East Greenland, Jan Mayen and East Iceland Currents.

As well as giving the voyage a more satisfying circular shape, this would give me a good reason for a third visit to Jan Mayen. Despite two previous visits, much of the island was still a mystery to me. I had yet to see its seven thousand foot volcanic peak, Mount Beerenberg, fully revealed. I had not yet explored the west coast. It is an island I am particularly fond of; it exerts a kind of magnetism. If at all possible, then, I would try to include it in the homeward trajectory.

The final consideration was the timing of my departure. This had to be finely judged. If I left too early I risked meeting too much ice too far south. If I left too late I risked meeting unfriendly autumnal weather and darker nights. The best time to be in the high Arctic from a weather point of view is July, but the ice does not reach its minimum values, usually, until well on in September.

A compromise therefore has to be made. I decided that I would leave a little later than my previous Arctic voyages, round about the beginning of July. This would put me at my most northerly point towards the end of the month or the beginning of August. This was a little early from an ice perspective, but at least meant I could complete the voyage in reasonable weather and without long dark nights.

I now had the theoretical shape of the voyage and its possible options clearly established. How it would turn out in practice was a different matter. There was only one way to find out.

Killer Whale

4

On a damp Sunday evening on the twenty-second of June I pulled up in front of the Whitehills harbourmaster's office, with *Mingming II* in tow. Apart from a couple of short comfort breaks we had been on the road for thirteen and a half hours.

It had been a long haul, not helped by some monsoon-like downpours as we negotiated the hilly Aberdeen ring road. I was tired. Whitehills, though, the tiny fishing harbour on the southern fringe of north-east Scotland's Moray Firth, and the departure point for my Arctic voyages, had become a second home to me, and I was revived immediately by the warmth of my welcome. I had not neglected the village during the two summers I had been boat-building. Brenda and I had gone up each year for the Whitehills regatta, and for the occasional weekend in winter. The friendships I had made had grown stronger.

Harbour commissioner Jimmy Forbes had already

ordered the crane; harbourmaster Bertie Milne supervised the lift-in, and by early afternoon the next day *Mingming II* was afloat and rigged.

'*Welcome home, Roger!*' The booming voice of the vice-chairman of the harbour commissioners Willy Milne rang out across the pontoon. Willy is the skipper of the Sun Odyssey 26 *Ambition*, and like so many of the Whitehills berth-holders, is a professional seaman. He has moved on from handling fishing boats to handling oil rigs. He offered to tow us out when the time came. So too did George Craigen, skipper of the Bavaria 32 *About Time*. George was once a ship's master on oil rig supply boats; now he directs their movements around the oil-fields. Another offer of a tow came from Alasdair Ramsay, local builder and developer, and skipper of the Westerly Centaur *Tanwood*.

We had been allotted a temporary berth alongside James Cowie's Dehler 36 *Sunrise*. This is a yacht which sparkles from its regular polishings, and which put to shame *Mingming II's* general air of scruffiness. James too is a man of the sea. Once employed on the oil rig stand-by ships he is now a marine superintendent and clearly a man for whom everything must be just so.

My old friend Jim Abel, retired fishing skipper and the relief harbourmaster at the time of my first voyage from Whitehills, came down to see me. He showed me his wounds: since my last visit he had been shot. Jim, who now occupies his time with his dogs and his pigeons, helps out at one of the local shoots. A wealthy industrialist, too quick on the trigger, had peppered Jim instead of the bird he was swinging for. Luckily Jim was side on, and got off with his right hand and lower arm riddled with lead. Many months on it was still not a pretty sight.

The harbour is overlooked by a steep hill that leads to the Knock Head bluff. The villagers have built a stepped path up the hill, and placed benches along the top. On a fine summer's evening it is a gathering place to sit and yarn and to look out over the wide waters of the firth to the mountains of Helmsdale away to the north-west. I took many a stroll up there and often sat and chatted with harbour commissioner Alastair Wiseman. Alastair too has re-invented himself. Once a much-respected fishing skipper, he now teaches marine search and rescue techniques in Aberdeen. The masters and mates of oil rig standby vessels come from all over the world to get their accreditation on his courses. Alastair has charge of a ship's bridge deck simulator which can re-create ocean conditions up to a storm Force 10.

It was a pleasure and a privilege to be in the company of these men for whom the sea is the only way of life. They probably still thought that I was a link or two short of an anchor chain: why would anyone even contemplate sailing to the Arctic in such small and engine-less yachts? Why, in fact, would anyone contemplate sailing to the Arctic in *any* sort of yacht? The men of Whitehills are practical, unsentimental men not much given to my kind of romantic foolishness. I sensed, though, that over the years I had at least earned a sliver of respect. They knew the sea and they knew what such voyages demanded.

The wind had settled in hard from the north-east, and so I was confined to port until the weather changed. This was no hardship, as I was in no hurry to leave. The daily ice-maps were not encouraging: the pack-ice, for some reason, was receding much less quickly than in the two previous years. Kong Karls Land and the sea to its east and west were still completely ice-bound. Further east, towards the islands of Franz Josef Land, the ice bulged to the south well into the Barents Sea.

I occupied myself with a list of jobs to improve the rig. I had noticed during our sailing trials that the carbon fibre sail battens were prone to chafe where they rubbed against the mast. They also clanked against the aluminium with a rather hard and ugly sound. I bought a long length of cheap, soft rope at the Macduff chandlery and served each batten, and the yard and boom, with a tight rope binding in way of the mast. I checked every lashing on the sail, and put a couple of stitches in every reef knot to ensure it held. Finally I made sure that every rope-end on board was properly whipped.

I worked hard too at the stowage, refining the positioning of everything and improving the lashings for the heavier items. At the back of my log book I made a big sketch of the boat, with every single stowage space on it, and recorded where everything was. This later proved invaluable, both for locating things quickly and for checking the rate of consumption of my stores.

I had a little time off. The Banff builder John Walker, who had converted the old Whitehills lifeboat shed, a monumental stone structure, into an exquisite residence, took me on a drive up the wooded hills of the Deveron Valley. It was beautiful countryside that surprised me with its steep ravines and twisting river. My mind was only half there, though. By now I was ready to set sail and was computing weather systems and ice movements and revising the myriad details that a thorough preparation demands.

The weather was still messy and uncertain, but it seemed that the prolonged north-easterly was about to blow itself out. It seemed too that I was unlikely to get an ideal run of conditions for departure: a settled favourable wind, that is, which would propel us clear of land, oil rigs and commercial traffic within two to three days. Well, I would just have to make the best of it.

On the morning of the fourth of July, with the forecast still uncertain, but with east to south-easterly winds in prospect, I decided it was time to go. Harbourmaster Bertie Milne offered to tow us out with his son-in-law's open dory *Swee'Pea*. It was a simple affair to throw a line for his crewman Graeme Gordon to hold. Alasdair Ramsay let go our shorelines and we were off.

Drawn on by little *Swee'Pea*, we eased smoothly through the outer basin, made a sharp turn to starboard out into the harbour channel and along the sea wall. The leftover swell from the north-east gave the first intimations that soon we would be at sea for real. Once clear of the channel I raised a couple of panels of sail and hauled in our tow-line. Another three panels had us moving easily in a fresh breeze from the south-east. Bertie, a keen photographer, circled us a few times and recorded the moment. *Mingming II*, at her best with the wind on her starboard quarter, settled quickly to her work.

We pulled away to the north. It was the greyest of days above and below. Only *Mingming II's* sun and moon insignia infused the world with any hint of brightness. *Swee'Pea* fell rapidly astern. I set the self-steering, climbed down into the hatchway, and listened. There it was once more, the music of the sea, the music, perhaps, of my life: water gurgling and slapping and hissing as we raced on, curving our wake to a galaxy of bubbles.

long-tailed Skua

5

Comfort is a relative concept. One man's luxury is another man's privation, and vice versa. Aboard *Mingming* I had, for the most part, felt supremely comfortable. I had a pallet six feet long and fifteen inches wide, thinly cushioned, on which I could lay myself out to sleep. I had a stove, a table, light, warmth, food and water. Everything was within easy reach. I could keep myself dry and secure. What's more, I could journey, taking my few necessities with me, and at no cost save my time and energy, wherever I wanted. Compared to most on this planet, I lived like a king.

I was now at sea for the first time aboard *Mingming II* in her finished state. I had not built her with an eye to more comfort for myself, but to create a marginally quicker, more efficient yacht. My main focus had been on an increased waterline length and a more powerful rig. This by definition meant a bigger structure. I could now feel, for the first time, the by-products of that extra size.

Ducking through the hatchway into the main cabin, I was almost embarrassed by the acres of luxury stretching to port and to starboard and forward to the watertight bulkhead. Deep-cushioned and richly upholstered bunks lay on either hand. I could sit here, or there, or perhaps over there, or on the wide companionway step, it too boasting a custom-made cushion. Half bulkheads divided the forward section from the main cabin, creating, in effect, two separate rooms. Later I improvised a make-shift curtain between the two, to stop heat escaping forward, and this reinforced the multiplex feel. The cabin sole was now a dance floor, a bowling alley, a path on which a man could take long walks, admiring the interior appointments as he went. All in all, there was room to swing several cats, without too much damage to swinger or swung.

That, though, was by no means the end of it. In my stockinged feet, my usual sea-wear, I could stand proud and indisputably *Homo erectus* under the observation pod. While thus standing, or if I felt like it, lounging with my arms resting on the shelf made by a retained section of the previous coach roof, I could watch the whole wide world in all its watery detail. Within a few seconds I realised what a boon this was going to be. I had wondered whether too much heel or a proper sea-going motion might limit the observation pod's effectiveness, but not a bit of it. Here was a fully three-dimensional three hundred and sixty degree window on the ocean, available at all times, in all weathers. To access it all I had to do was to stand up.

Then there were the hatches, and the light they delivered. Three hatches created three possible exit points, three skylights, three ventilation ports. After so many years spent below *Mingming's* single hatch I was now thrice blessed. The hatches created a fairly even flood of illumination fore and aft and so, despite the deliberately subdued interior colour scheme, *Mingming II* felt light and airy.

It was all too much; too much un-allayed luxury. What had happened to simplicity? Where had minimalism gone? I had to be careful: this high life could become addictive. Much more of it and I might be tempted to buy a spare plastic mug, or upgrade my toilet bucket, or invest in a pair of gloves.

We raced easily on to the north-north-east, now down to three panels as we moved away from the shelter of the Moray coast. A big and purposeful tugboat, the *Ems*, passed close across our stern, heading west. I ate some fresh bread and cheese, and a banana, for my lunch. It would be a few days until I took up my regular sea-going diet. Fresh bread would be replaced by vacuum-packed pumpernickel; bananas by green apples.

Rain lowered down to sea level, veiling the world. My first impression, as we moved further offshore, was that *Mingming II* was, if anything, slightly less sedate in her movements than *Mingming*. Her roll was a little more severe, her feel marginally more hard-edged. There was not much in it, though. I was freshly back at sea, in any case, and not yet fully re-assimilated to the constant motion aboard. One thing was for certain: *Mingming II* was a more vocal ship. The new woodwork of the after cabin and bridge deck creaked and groaned with each roll. It was a reassuring sound: the incessant talk of a timber ship.

On the other hand *Mingming II* was quieter through the water, with no slapping under the quarter. I made some notes on all of this in the log: the start of a long process of discovery and analysis.

I thought again about discomfort, and concluded that it has less to do with physical causality than with mental interpretation. It is what the Stoics would call a 'wrong impression': an unfiltered reaction to stimuli beyond the mind. I made another note to myself to remember this next time I felt cold and wet.

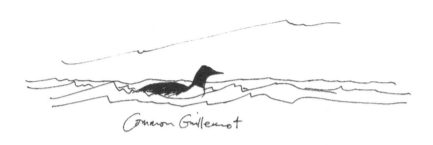

Common Guillemot

6

We had cleared the coast in a beneficent breeze on the quarter, but weather is weather, and it did not last. After a complete about-face to the north-west, forcing us hard on the wind for a few hours, conditions eased with an alarming rapidity. By eleven o'clock in the evening we were becalmed.

It was a violent calm. The north-east swell, pumped up by a good ten days' worth of muscular wind from that quarter, was rolling through, hard and undiminished, throwing *Mingming II* to port and to starboard every few seconds. I was shocked by the severity of the motion, a steely-edged and unrelenting whiplash. Each lurch threw all my stores just a fraction one way or the other, creating a collective and mighty *crrrump*. I lashed the sail bundle tightly to the boom gallows and strapped myself to the starboard berth. Sleep was impossible.

For a while my affection for *Mingming II* faltered. The noise and motion was hellish, and I blamed the boat. It seemed that her ballast ratio was too high, forcing her back upright too quickly and creating a self-sustaining pendulum effect. This voyage would undoubtedly bring many long periods of calm weather; I was dismayed at the prospect of having to endure this kind of treatment time after time.

I tried to remember whether *Mingming* had ever been as bad in a calm. She had, of course, but three years away from the sea had put a softer, rosier tint on my memories. Now she could do no wrong. For an hour or two I wondered whether I had done the right thing to replace her.

As the night went on and the swell started to ease, so the motion relented. I managed a few hours sleep on and off and felt a little better about *Mingming II*. She was undoubtedly a stiffer and less gentle mover than *Mingming*, but her appalling motion had been down as much as anything to the sea state. It happens from time to time: the wave period and amplitude is just right to generate the maximum roll in a particular hull form. Poor old *Mingming II;* she had met the worst conditions first time out.

My doubts about her were quickly dispelled. The slightest of puffs, a scarcely discernible movement of air, came up from the north-east and I raised six panels of the sail. *Mingming II* responded to the challenge, ghosting smoothly forward over the glassy heave of the sea. Now she was in her element; *Mingming* would never have made progress in such a faint breeze.

The various post-modern structures of the Captain oil field moved slowly astern to our east. Groups of guillemots and fulmars peppered the sea. A ship crossed ahead, hull down and heading east. It was a chilly morning, despite the clearing sky, but I left the after hatch open; the sooner I started to acclimatise to colder weather the better.

The breeze, still faint, veered to east-south-east and we crept steadily on, with just a smattering of bubbles to mark our passage. Mid-afternoon the fin of a lone male killer whale passed astern and I watched the efforts of a stowaway spider as it diligently spun a web under the stern navigation light. I felt a great sadness for this spider. It was doing what it was compelled to do, ignorant of the uselessness of its hard work. It would never again catch a fly, would never again eat. Soon it would be dead.

The breeze came in more strongly, bringing with it a mass of broken low cloud, and by four the next morning the dark smudge of Fair Isle was visible on our port bow. The direct course to Bjørnøya led past the east of the Shetlands, and for a while I kept us well up to windward to be sure of a good margin past the islands' southerly headland, Sumburgh Head. The sky was changing rapidly, though, and I did not like the look of it. High cirrus fanned out from the south. Lower down, ragged grey cloud raced along on a building wind. We were clearly in for a hard blow, almost certainly from the east. My aversion to lee shores kicked in and just after noon on the sixth of July, a little more than two days out from Whitehills, I decided to bear off and run through the northern passage of the Fair Isle Channel and up the west side of the Shetlands.

It was the right decision. The short night brought brutal squalls that had us down to a single panel of sail. There was a certain comfort in having nothing but clear ocean under our lee. I ran out into the North Atlantic for a few hours, to be sure of a good clearance of the Shetlands' most westerly island, Foula, before resuming our northerly course. By six the next morning the stark seaward cliffs of Foula were abeam.

I was disturbed by how little bird life there was. We were just a mile or two from one of the major breeding grounds. Not so long ago the summer air here was thick with squadrons of gannets and busy flocks of auks. There were terns and shearwaters too, and petrels, skuas and fulmars. The place should have been teeming with life intent on its reproduction. Now there was little more than the occasional straggling gannet and a puffin or two. The skies resounded with an eloquent emptiness.

The half gale was short and sharp and quickly gone. As we pulled away from Foula and shaped our definitive, unimpeded course for Bjørnøya, the skies cleared and the wind eased to a perfect quartering Force 5.

It is hard to imagine a finer afternoon of sailing. For a start we were now freed up from the constraints of land. The whalebacks of northern Shetland still dominated the distant eastern horizon, but they were now no more than agreeable windward scenery. Ahead lay a thousand miles of open sea. Above, the sky had opened to a piercing blue that had the sea shimmering and sparkling. With just three panels set, a rock-solid and comforting configuration, *Mingming II* settled to her work with perfect balance and an easy stride. Stirred by the beauty of the moment I exited the hatch to record it on film. This, though, was not enough; I wanted to integrate myself more physically into the scene, to become participant as well as spectator. I unhooked the self-steering chain and took control of the helm. For the sheer pleasure of it I sat for an hour or two in the cockpit and hand-steered. Now I had a full and indissoluble connection to *Mingming II* and to the sea that we were prancing through and to the wind that was blowing and to the radiating sun. All were conjoined in an act of the utmost physicality. It was somehow about movement and energy, life, *joie de vivre. Mingming II* bent to the wind, hummed forward and through the tiller I could feel every nuance of her movement and will and driving force. It needed nothing more than the lightest fingertip touch to keep her bounding on. Thus subsumed into the holy continuum of sun, sky, sea and sail, I caressed *Mingming II* northwards.

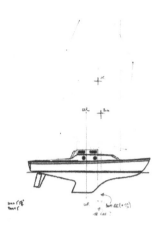

7

There is a common misconception that the further one sails north, the worse the weather. During the summer months, this is not the case. I knew well enough that once we had passed through the band of depressions whisked across the North Atlantic by the jet stream, we would emerge into a wide area of what I think of as intermediate weather. Further north still we would meet predominantly high pressure with its light winds and clear skies.

The boundaries between these three distinct tranches of weather are of course in constant flux. The determining factor is principally the position, at any one time, of the northern hemisphere polar jet stream, a wide band of fast-moving air high in the atmosphere. This is an unpredictable phenomenon. During the summer months it generally moves north a little, delivering its worst packages to the north of the British Isles. From time to time, as has happened in recent years, it does not follow this pattern, remaining further south and ruining many a European's summer holiday.

Over the years I have come to the opinion that by about 66°North, at roughly the Arctic Circle, one is usually well clear of the constant storms generated by the jet stream. My strategy is always to sail north as quickly and directly as possible to reach this latitude. From there on the chances of meeting really destructive weather are much reduced. In heading to the Arctic Circle I have in mind another staging point at 62°North. This latitude has navigational rather than meteorological significance. The Scottish and Norwegian oil fields extend, in the North Sea, to this latitude. As long as I have kept well to the west of them it is only at 62°North that I feel I have attained the kind of sea room that I prefer. It is only then that I can fully relax and settle in to the business of pure pelagic sailing.

As a rule of thumb, the intermediate phase spans about ten degrees of latitude, six hundred nautical miles, between 66°North and 76°North. This is usually an area of good sailing in miserable conditions. Winds blow generally at a steady Force 5 to 6, sometimes a little less, sometimes a little more. Directions vary, but winds from north-west to north-east are common. The sky is usually overcast; fog is the rule rather than the exception; rain is not unknown. Full-blown storms are a rarity. The few I have encountered in these latitudes tend to be short-lived.

For six hundred miles, once the Arctic Circle has been crossed, it is a case of getting on with the business of making one's northing in a rather dour and workman-like way. Grey and foggy day follows grey and foggy day. It gets colder too, of course.

Eventually the reward for all this humdrum voyaging will be earned. The great prize at the end of it is the emergence into the Arctic High. By 76°North the North Pole is less than eight hundred and fifty miles away, but many a day will be spent basking under a warmish sun, whether at two in the afternoon or two in the morning. Winds are generally light and fickle. Calms abound. When a breeze does get up it will tend to be uncertain and squally. The light has a different quality from further south, no doubt because of the strange angle of the sun. Bizarre cloud formations appear then melt away. Nothing is quite as it should be. There is something deeply seductive about this other-worldliness.

With a long voyage ahead it is useful to have it thus broken down into several phases. The immediate targets are less daunting. Sailing such a direct south-north trajectory, the individual degrees of latitude provide another easily achievable measure of progress. As long as there is some sort of wind, every twenty-four hours should notch up another degree. Two in one day, a hundred and twenty miles of sailing, is a little ambitious, but three degrees over a forty-eight hour period is possible. Ticking off the degrees of latitude, whether sailing north or south, becomes a central navigational theme, generating a note in the log, and sometimes a minor treat for the hard-working skipper.

The voyage's first major leg, eleven hundred and twenty miles from Whitehills to Bjørnøya, was composed, therefore, of a series of much smaller distances. At any one moment I concentrated first on the next degree of latitude, next on the intermediary targets of 62°North and 66°North. In this way I never felt overwhelmed by the distances in prospect, or discouraged if progress was slow.

There was nothing discouraging about our departure from the Shetlands. The breeze blew steadily from the south-east. The sky, apart from some towering white columns of cumulus rising over the last of the islands to the east, remained a pristine blue. The sea still sparkled and *Mingming II* sped easily on. We passed close by a stationary ship, perhaps surveying for oil. By early evening Muckle Flugga lighthouse was visible on the starboard beam. For a change of connection with the boat I sat on the portable seat I had made for the bridge deck and steered with the hand lines. I was, in this configuration, sitting very comfortably half-in and half-out of the after hatch, with my feet on the top companionway step. This gave me the best of both worlds: participation in the sensuous physicality of the moment combined with the security of the cabin.

I thought back to previous voyages. This was now the fourth departure from the Shetlands. It had become something of a habit, and so was bound about with the reassurance and mundanity of the habitual. Seven years earlier, when we had first passed Muckle Flugga bound for the Faroes and Iceland, this northerly outpost had seemed grandiosely Nordic and outlandish. In the intervening years it had somehow shrunk in stature and effect. I had seen too many distant and truly Arctic mountains and buttresses and glaciers to be overawed by such a tame southern copy.

By nine that evening the topmost curve of Unst was sinking quickly to the horizon. We had been at sea for three and a half days. Aboard *Mingming II* I felt supremely comfortable and at ease. A rare afternoon of hand-steering had cemented our partnership. With the land almost gone our first adventure together was properly under way.

8

It had been a long and hard haul to get to this point: three years of thinking, planning and relentless physical work. I had experienced many a moment of doubt. Was it all going to be worth it? Was the rig going to perform as intended? Would I ever manage to get the boat ready for sea? Was the whole project a misconception?

We live in a very connected global village and I had received many unsolicited comments about *Mingming II* from complete strangers all over the world. Most were supportive of what I was doing, but there were detractors too. I was told in no uncertain terms that the mast would fail; that the aluminium was the wrong temper and would soon bend or break. I was told that the hinged sail would be inefficient, that the triple keels would slow the boat down, that the observation pod would make her top heavy, and so on. I had enough belief in my own convictions not to be unsettled by these negative comments. I was not in the least interested in what other people might think. This was not based on arrogance, but on the fundamental principle of creating the yacht purely from my own mental and physical resources. This was for two quite distinct reasons.

The first relates to a fierce adherence to the concept of total personal responsibility in all things. I refuse to subscribe to the growing culture of complaint, blame and victimhood. I try to live by a very simple creed: *do not wish; do not expect; do not complain.* Although not an easy philosophy to follow to the letter, it has a strongly grounding, calming effect. It keeps one centred on the immediate moment and on one's own capacities. It demands self-sufficiency. For an ocean sailor there is no better ideal.

The second reason for insulating the project against outside input was aesthetic rather than philosophical. I had come to view my sailing activities as a loose kind of performance art: create a yacht; create a voyage; create a written account. Each of the three aspects of this process requires a quite different set of skills and a different kind of application, but they are all tightly bound together. Each stage flows into the next stage and refers back to the previous stage. The quality, and the success or failure of each, informs the other two. Art is coherence, and it is of fundamental importance, therefore, to maintain a coherent approach to the three stages of building, sailing and writing. Just as I sail singlehanded and with total self-sufficiency, and just as I write alone and without editorial help, so I have to design and build as independently as possible. Not to do so would destroy the coherency of the whole.

There are other benefits to this approach. From a purely practical perspective, it means that I have an intimate connection to every detail of the physical construction of the boat and the thinking behind it. I have a clear mental image of what lies behind every bulkhead and panel, or under every layer of paint or fibreglass. I know what has been bolted, what has been nailed, what has been screwed. I know what can be taken apart and what cannot. I know the relative strength of all the components of the structure. Any problems that arise can be solved quickly and with confidence.

I can therefore go to sea with a relaxed frame of mind. As I know the structure in its entirety, and have total confidence in it, there are no questionable areas. I have no nagging fear of an unforeseen and perhaps insoluble problem. Add to that the inherent softness and lack of stress of the junk rig and you have a formula for worry-free ocean sailing.

The other great side-benefit of creating one's own boat is the sheer enjoyment and satisfaction that comes from sailing it. As we pulled away from the last of the land I thought back to the single sketch plan I had made, two and a half years previously, of *Mingming II's* proposed sail plan and coach roof alterations. This was the only drawing for the re-build: just a few lines on a sheet of paper. It included the necessary calculations for the positioning of the new rig, an outline of the sail and a rough sketch of the observation pod, new after hatch and remodelled cabin sides. Now here it all was, transformed from an aspirational drawing to an actual deep-sea cruiser. Old lengths of timber, sheets of plywood, rolls of sail-cloth and fibreglass, cans of epoxy, tins of paint, a thousand screw and bolts, and a municipal lamp post had been cut and sawn and sewn and reconfigured and rejoined to form this yacht gambolling gaily northwards. It had all come from my own head and my own hands, and it seemed almost miraculous. The joy I felt was in direct proportion to the effort I had made. The sail curved to the wind and pulled us smoothly along. Every stitch was my own. The outrageously-conceived mast rose sturdily to the skies with a graceful taper and unbending intent. The balance and harmony of the whole infused my own state of mind. *Mingming II* had become an extension of my inner self, the physical expression of a lifetime's yearning. She satisfied the two overwhelming imperatives: to create and to voyage. She was all the better, too, for her singular appearance. Conceived with a view to uncompromising utility, she was odd-looking and stridently unconventional. I had made no attempt to prettify her. Utility, though, has its own aesthetic. She looked, in her own way, ferociously fit for purpose. There was an uplifting beauty to be found in this. It was not the beauty of sweet lines or subtle colour schemes. There was nothing here of the classical or the post-modern. She exuded, rather, a seductive air of blunt practicality.

That afternoon of idyllic sailing was a pivotal moment. Any reservations I may still have had about *Mingming II* were dispelled for good. She was all I had hoped for. We were not many miles from where I had sailed south, for the last time, in *Mingming*. For three years I had kept my future options open, in case *Mingming II* did not meet expectations. Henceforth there would be no doubt about it: *Mingming II* would replace *Mingming* permanently.

Long-tailed Skuas Attack Practice

9

The land fell away astern and we settled in to the task of making our northing. I did not intend to sail a straight-line course to Bjørnøya. My plan was to head more or less due north, only easing to the north-east towards Bjørnøya once we were past the North Cape of Norway. This would keep us well away from land, shallower water and the main shipping routes.

As night drew on the cloud came in. It arrived piecemeal, staking little claims here and there until it had overrun the clear sky beyond. By morning this southern sector of the Norwegian Sea had assumed its habitual decor of overbearing grey. For the next two weeks we would have no more than a rare glimpse of blue sky and sun.

The cloud came in and the wind dropped away. With six panels of the sail set *Mingming II* ghosted fluently on. I kept the seventh panel in reserve; it was only for use in the smoothest of seas when there was little chance of wringing stresses at the masthead. The turbo-charger was a mighty weapon, but it had to be brought into action with a certain restraint.

I watched a battle royal between an Arctic Skua and an Arctic Tern. Here were two masters of the air locked in a combat so quick and twisting that it was no easy matter to follow the fine detail of the engagement. The skua was chasing the tern, hoping to force it to give up its catch. The tern was as fast and agile as a swallow and used every aerobatic trick to shake itself free from its pursuer. At lightning speed it changed direction, looped, rolled, stalled, plunged, hovered and dived. The skua, in an extraordinary display of reactive follow-my-leader, mimicked every movement, just a few inches behind the tern. The skua was a larger, darker copy of the tern, sleek-winged and long-tailed, and so became a kind of doppelganger as it copied every nuance of the tern's flight. I have many times observed the doughtiness of the Arctic Tern. They may be fine-lined, graceful birds, but they have hearts of steel. A pair of Arctic Terns will often harry a skua with merciless aggression, taking turns to launch a withering attack. This tern was alone, and so at a disadvantage. Despite this, it was not going to cede. It could keep up this kind of virtuoso flying for much longer than the skua, which eventually tired of the chase and withdrew.

I took advantage of the light weather to stick myself through the forward hatch and clean the forward windows of the observation pod. I had breakfasted at six, as usual, but with all this breathless activity was feeling it was time for a little something. The formal eating routine for this voyage still had to be established, and so, as captain of the ship, and a magnanimous one at that, I ordered a ration of four squares of fruit and nut chocolate to be issued to all crewmembers at eight o'clock every morning.

The wind backed and freshened, driving *Mingming II*

northwards at a fine old pace: our noon position showed we had covered ninety miles over the previous twenty-four hours. After lunch I exited the hatch to deal with the voyage's first minor problem. The lines that lead from the self-steering gear to the tiller, and the small blocks through which they run, were chafing the cloth tops of the drogue bins. I sewed a sacrificial square of cloth to each bin cover, and lathered the cloth and the lines with lanolin. This put paid to the chafe for the rest of the voyage.

Mid-afternoon we crossed 62°North, a double milestone, as it put us in unequivocally clear water in all directions, and marked the halfway point to the Arctic Circle. The wind backed further, bringing us hard on the wind. Using the hand-held GPS to determine relative speeds, I experimented by sailing at different angles to the apparent wind. *Mingming II* would sail happily at 37.5°, making three and a half knots. Easing off to 45° her speed increased to four knots. Sailing slightly free she was at a better angle to the sea too, and less likely to stall. Sailing a junk rig to windward in anything of a sea requires the same approach as a gaff-rigged yacht: the priority is to maintain good boat speed. It is generally preferable, therefore, to ease off just a fraction.

Throughout a short night which was now little more than a darkish twilight the headwind blew harder, backing into the north-north-west and bringing with it a thickening mass of low cloud. Rain seemed inevitable. By seven o'clock it had started and by eleven it was torrential. With the shift of the wind we were bucking to windward straight into the steep seas left over from the day before. *Mingming II* plunged gamely on, shouldering great dollops of green water aft as she went. Warm and dry, and shod with no more than a pair of thick socks, I lounged under the observation pod and watched the rain lashing down. From time to time sea water thudded into the forward deadlights of the pod. After five days of easy sailing we were now into the hard graft of a long voyage.

It was a noisy, hard-edged advance through the waves, and so it took me a little while to pick up the strange whistling that overlay the creak and crash of our progress. I thought I was hallucinating, or maybe going mad. Once my ears had focussed on the proper frequencies, and cut out the mass of ambient white noise, there was no doubt about it: I could hear the most beautiful and unearthly warbling. Snatches of pure-toned melody hovered somewhere in the boat. *What the hell is that?* I checked my little radio receiver to see if it had somehow switched itself on. No, it was locked off and silent. Other voices added themselves to the tune, creating a weird counterpoint. A minor third repeated itself up and down, up and down, like some sort of ghostly police siren. I could not locate the source of the sound in the cabin; it seemed to radiate from the hull itself.

I looked aft and there was the answer. I really ought to have recognised what was happening, as this was not the first time I had heard this particular music. A pod of twenty or thirty pilot whales had joined us. They were leaping along in tight groupings, just aft of each quarter, singing as they went. Once again I was struck by the contrast between their brutish musculature and the finesse of their vocalisations. To my ears it was singing, or at least tuneful whistling. To them, no doubt, it was something more prosaic, neither music nor speech, but simple signals. Maybe the sounds had no implicit meaning at all. Perhaps they did no more than assert the whales' togetherness, establishing and reinforcing the relationships and hierarchies within the group. And yet...the sounds were so beautiful and so seductive, it was tempting to think that perhaps they sang for the pleasure of it, that it was a form of sensual entertainment. These pilot whales were, after all, closely packed and therefore in visual contact with each other. They were not down in the dark depths hunting. They had no need to vocalise to establish their relative positions, or to signal the presence of prey. They were not lone whales singing to attract mates. It seemed, therefore, that there could only be two reasons for them to be whistling so energetically: either they were engaging in what the sociolinguists call phatic communication, talking to each other simply to maintain their bonding, or else they were whistling for the sheer enjoyment of it. Maybe it was a mix of both.

10

The wind blew hard from the northerly quadrant, veering and backing and so keeping us shifting from one tack to the other to maintain the most advantageous heading. Sometimes it worked itself up to half a gale, but the periods of heavy gusts were short-lived. Mostly we sailed in a solid Force 5 to 6.

The days merged almost indistinguishably one into the next. The over-riding theme was a steely and oppressive grey that gripped closer and soon became thick fog. I was once again grateful for the observation pod, which enabled steady watch-keeping in this reduced world.

There was little to punctuate the blandness of the days. Two long-tailed skuas came in to examine us, followed the next day by a small pod of killer whales. One night I was startled by the blast of a foghorn. It was the evocative sound of my youth: foghorns on the River Mersey and its approaches, vessels to and from every corner of the globe announcing their presence on what was still a ship-laden stretch of water. Here now was an unusually conscientious skipper trumpeting away at the regulation interval. Perhaps it was a cruise ship giving reassurance to its passengers. The blasts seemed to pass close along our starboard side and were soon lost astern. The heavy traffic continued: next morning a second ship, modestly proportioned and with a single crane amidships, passed close to starboard, it too heading south.

The stern-light spider worked away. It had extended the structure of its web to include one of the self-steering lines as a bottom anchor. The web shimmered with drops of moisture culled from the foggy air. Nothing animate or edible had been trapped. I wondered where the spider derived its energy from, and how it could continue to produce the lengthening threads of silk that its expanding web required. We had been at sea for over a week and here it was, creating a masterful sculpture, and all the materials necessary to construct it, on an empty stomach.

The wind veered to east and then south-east, unlocking us from a head wind and a head sea and pushing our daily runs back up to ninety miles or so. The change of wind did nothing to drive off the fog, though, or the cooling air. I was still wearing light clothing: cotton sailing trousers, a cotton T-shirt and a lightweight fleece. My body sometimes complained at this modest swaddling; my mind ignored the complaints. It is a question of where the control lies. If allowed, the body will make constant and insistent demands: *I'm cold. I'm hot. I'm tired. I'm hungry…*and so on. The more the mind cedes to these complaints, the more shrill and self-confident they become. But if the mind says *No, No* and again *No*, the body will eventually relent: *OK, I didn't really mean it. No, I'm fine. I can get used to this. No problem.* There is a constant tussle between the two. The more the mind says *No*, the easier it becomes for it to keep on saying *No* and the less the body insists; it knows it is on a losing streak. Once the mind has established a permanent dominance, which us in effect what constitutes self-discipline, and practises this dominance regularly and consistently, life becomes much easier. One needs less, is able to endure more, and feels generally stronger and more controlled.

It was particularly important, as we were heading for the far north, to establish a high level of self-discipline early on. I ignored the coldness I felt and sure enough, after a few days, my body started to accept the status quo and to adapt to it. It was only when we crossed the Arctic Circle, at just after seven o'clock on the morning of the thirteenth of July, and after nine days at sea, that I upgraded the flimsy summer clothing that I been wearing since our departure. I put on long woollen underwear and tracksuit top and bottoms. The tracksuit was cotton, but heavier than the trousers and fleece I had been wearing. For an hour or two we had some rare blue sky, marred only by a layer of high mackerel cloud, and newly decked out as I was in all this warm finery, I felt hot and uncomfortable. I was able to maintain this level of clothing up to our highest latitude.

The sunny period was short-lived: after a couple of hours we were back to fog and a strengthening wind from the east-north-east. I was warm, but it was clear that the falling temperatures were affecting the cabin: the aluminium frames of the central and forward hatches were creating condensation. This was the only moisture inside the boat; the bilge was totally dry. It could have been annoying, as the central hatch condensation occasionally dripped onto the leeward berth, where I usually had my bedding, but I just ignored it. It was fresh water that dries quickly and cleanly. It was harmless and quickly gone. It is sea water and its persistent damp stickiness that I make every effort to exclude from inside.

The crossing of the Arctic Circle, with its attendant filming and a celebratory blast on the ship's foghorn, created a brief highpoint in the flat and unchanging day-to-day topography. It also marked the halfway point to Bjørnøya. We were now unequivocally at sea and getting somewhere.

The easterly wind cranked itself up, forcing us down to one panel of sail and encouraging the occasional wave to deliver a thundering blow on the beam. Banks of cold fog rolled in. I slept in short spells throughout the night. As ever, sleep was forbidden between six in the morning and midday. The first northern phase fulmar of the voyage, a sombre, mucky-plumaged version of its southern cousins, and an out-rider of the high Arctic, joined our avian escort. Rain came in for a while. The rain was replaced with hazy sunshine before the next round of fog took over. With each change the wind shifted slightly, and dropped or strengthened, and so I was always at the hatch, raising or lowering sail and adjusting the self-steering gear. I made a rare exit of the hatch to tighten a nut on the rudder stock which had somehow loosened itself. The wind went round to the west, clearing away the fog but making no impression on the encircling grey. The westerly blew harder and with just a couple of panels set we raced north, recording another eighty-five miles noon-to-noon. For some reason my right rib cage started to ache; maybe it was my Davis Strait war wound re-asserting itself. I ignored it and raised more sail as the westerly started to fade. By nine in the evening of the sixteenth of July, with 70°North well astern, we were comprehensively becalmed. I lowered the sail and lashed it firmly to the boom gallows. A large sun shone weakly through the cloud cover. *Mingming II* moved sweetly to the swell, dispelling a latent fear. Snug in the Arctic and happy as only a lone sailor can be, I slept.

11

To stay at sea; that is the thing. To stay at sea and become, provisionally, a creature of the sea. To encapsulate oneself upon it. To learn to accept its harshness. To give oneself up to its great metaphor. To absorb the constancy of its change. To become part of its endless cycle. To grow easy with its whims. To see it as the life it is. To learn patience. To exorcise fear. To understand that it is no better and no worse. To grow stronger on it. To rise above the merely terrestrial. To confront the ultimate solitude of mind. To value un-attachment. To pass by peopled rocks, unmoved. To lose oneself in the journey, the voyage. To think of nothing but today's sea and today's sky. To know that every adverse wind contains a hidden gift. To love the encircling fulmars. To respect the whale as one might an innocent deity. To learn openness. To find a way to oneself. To excise the nonsense. To keep faith with the sea, even when forced back to the soil and the concrete.

Minke Whale ~ First Phase in Surfacing Sequence.

12

For twenty hours we lay there, waiting for a wind. A dozen or so fulmars joined us, dozing off the stern and occasionally bickering amongst themselves. One paddled in close and we held a one-sided conversation. It was the usual thing: I asked him where he was from, how the family was, where he was off for his holidays and so on. He did not answer, just cocked his head and stared back at me. I tried another line of approach, squawking loudly at him a couple of times. Once again there was no reaction.

I thought I heard a soft effusion of whale breath somewhere, but could not locate its source.

The spider's web had been washed away in the last bout of heavier weather. I had assumed the spider had gone too, but here it was again, constructing a new web from scratch. For a while I could not decide whether this tenacity was noble or stupid, but concluded that it was neither: a genetic imperative has no moral aspect. The biosphere is no more and no less than a zillion, zillion organisms, man included, getting on with the pre-programmed business of killing, eating and reproducing. The strategies might vary, but not the genetic compulsion. We are all in the same boat on that one.

Thus becalmed I had assumed that we would still be pushed north on the North Atlantic Current. Studying the hand-held GPS a little longer than usual, when establishing our noon position, I could see that this was not the case. We must have landed in a back-eddy that was carrying us slightly south of west. This partly explained our limited progress over the previous twenty-four hours: a mere sixteen nautical miles.

Another sighing breath seemed to come from somewhere ahead, and there it was at last: a lone minke whale doing the rounds. It was the first of many which, during the frequent calms of this voyage, would investigate us from a discreet distance, circling around for hour after hour. The radius of these gyrations sometimes contracted, sometimes expanded, but we were always at their centre point. I hoped that one might come right in and lie alongside and commune with us for while, but it never happened.

Late in the afternoon a faint zephyr started up from the south. It was a scarcely discernible movement of air, but with the need to be getting on, and with the sea now reduced to a gentle heave, I wondered about setting all seven panels of the sail. This was not a decision I could make on my own; to unleash the full power of the Triple H TB just like that, on an unsuspecting ocean, requires adherence to regulatory procedures and the full agreement of the ship's complement. I therefore issued an executive order summoning the whole crew to assemble forthwith. Out they crawled, one by one, and a sorry, disreputable bunch they were. Here was the Ship's Boy, whose presence aboard I had almost forgotten. With no foredeck work to do he was almost redundant, a gleeful state of affairs from his perspective. It seemed he was spending his time dosing somewhere in the forward cabin, confining his activity to scratching himself and picking his nose. Next came the Ship's Doctor *and* Dentist, a prissy, self-important pseudo-medic if ever there was. In his own modest eyes he was second only to Hippocrates in the annals of medical history, and was consequently scandalised at being forced to consider a question of mere seamanship. Finally, out of the darkest recesses, shuffled the pale and skeletal figure of the Ship's Collector of Rain. What can one say about a man whose sole obsession is with tubes, bottles, plastic containers and the calculation of volumes to the millilitre? They shifted and mumbled, avoiding all eye contact, as I explained the situation. It was scarcely Ahab grasping the forward rail of the quarter deck and haranguing his men with promises of gold pieces. This is, after all, the twenty-first century; what was required was a stakeholder consensus. This was achieved through telepathy rather than open discussion, and so, crew dismissed back to their various unsavoury lairs, I set about raising the full sail.

This was a stop-start process. After each couple of panels I cleated the main halyard, to give myself a few seconds rest, and to make sure that the mainsheet and parrels were free to run for the next lift. The main sheet could occasionally be troublesome: with so many blocks attaching it to the pulpit and the sheet spans it had a tendency to twist on itself, and so needed manually overhauling to keep it free to run. The final, seventh panel required some physical effort to raise, with the whole weight of the yard, sail, battens and boom now brought into play. The masthead and yard blocks had to be brought within an inch or two of each other to achieve a good set of the sail, bringing the centre of the yard itself almost to the masthead.

It was a relatively demanding operation, then, to set the

whole awesome acreage of the Triple H TB. It was worth the effort, though. The rig, broad and uncompromising, towered into the grey murk above, and with its height and its area soon harnessed the faint breeze that had started up. With the wind almost astern *Mingmng II* powered steadily forward, fomenting a consistent wake of frothy bubbles and sending out the occasional hiss and gurgle as she moved through the ambient swell. Some magic seemed to be at work here, for *Mingming II's* forward progress cancelled out, at deck level, the movement of air from astern. We were gliding forwards in a bubble of total calm, transported to the heart of a poem:

The helmsman steered, the ship moved on;
Yet never a breeze up blew...

I knew well enough that it was not a spirit nine fathom deep propelling us along, but the stronger breeze aloft. I had to steer, though; with the apparent wind nullified to zero the self-steering gear could not operate. I sat in the hatchway and steered with lines, preferring where possible to use some feature of the sky as a guide, rather than the compass. This was easier on my eyes and generally more pleasant.

For the best part of two hours *Mingming II* showed off her light weather talents, conjuring up motion out of nothing and seemingly confounding the laws of physics. What a pleasure it was, to race along in such contradictory stillness.

The wind backed and strengthened. I reduced sail to six panels and connected the self-steering gear. Thus released from the tyranny of the tiller, I cooked my evening meal. With the perfect combination of a beam wind and a following sea we drove on northwards.

Dolphin Acrobatics

13

By nine-thirty the following morning we had been at sea for two weeks. I noted in the log that these two weeks had passed relatively quickly and uneventfully. I could now feel the weight of experience, the accrued benefit of so many thousands of sea miles, with the resultant balance between know-how, reasonable expectation, mental control and physical hardiness. *Mingming II* had so far been all I had hoped for: quick, handy, light on the helm and comfortable. I noted too that the observation pod, allowing as it did a constant monitoring of the surrounding seascape, added a whole new dimension to the experience.

I thought more about the pod, and realised that it could provide the basis of a business opportunity. With a bit of entrepreneurial imagination I could make a fortune! Yes indeed, if I played things right I could soon be rich, and retire to an apartment in Marbella; one with a balcony and a sea view! I could buy a wide-screen television and a dishwasher! I could drive around in a shiny convertible with a blonde Russian girlfriend caressing the back of my neck! All I needed were a couple of dozen fee-paying passengers, and the key to this was the pod:

> *Welcome aboard! Enjoy spectacular views of northern seas thanks to the Mingming II Kroozeliner™ Observation Pod! Passengers can experience panoramic vistas of the Arctic Ocean while staying warm and dry (hot drinks and canapés served on demand). The KOP™ offers standing space for lounging and observing, and for the added comfort of our more elderly passengers custom-designed padded seating is available. From the unsurpassed luxury of the KOP™ see amazing sights of icebergs, hump-backed whales, storm-flecked waves, polar bears and walruses. Watch real sailors pull on ropes! Gold-package ticket-holders may also dine with the Captain (Terms and Conditions apply).*

This was without doubt a terrific business plan. It needed a little more work, perhaps, but it reflected what was by now a deep-seated appreciation of this boxy appendage; it really had transformed the character of our voyages.

We were of course still a long way from the Arctic Ocean itself, but that morning we crossed 71°North. This was not insignificant. Directly to our east, a few hundred miles away, lay the North Cape of Norway; a somewhat longer sail due west would bring us to Jan Mayen. We were thus shaking off the last headland of continental Europe and its last stray island. All that now remained between us and the Arctic pack-ice was the Svalbard archipelago. We were moving too into the Greenland Sea. I have never been able to determine whether there is a precise boundary between this final stretch of water before the Arctic Ocean and the more southerly Norwegian Sea, but 71°North or thereabouts seems the logical latitude.

On we moved in a round of light winds, fog and occasional clear patches. I exited the hatch to lubricate the self-steering gear and thereby encourage it to be more responsive in these gentle conditions. I watched an aeronautical training session as an adult long-tailed skua put its offspring through its paces, chasing it nose to tail, up, down and all around with lightning twists and turns, before reversing roles and getting young Harry to play the harrier. An Arctic tern tried to perch on the masthead, but even in a subdued sea a masthead is an awkward, rotating, lurching, treacherous kind of landing pad and the tern soon gave up. A juvenile Sabine's gull, a herald of the high Arctic, and exquisitely plumaged in white, grey and inky black, joined our fulmar escort for a while. I made a sketch of it in the ship's log, and, on the facing page, one of the great skua that passed ahead of us the following day.

In the meantime, the observation pod had attracted its first passenger. Our stowaway spider had abandoned his hunting ground at the stern and made his way forward. Now he was busily at work in the aft corner of the observation pod's forward port deadlight. I could watch him from a few inches away through the polycarbonate window. He was a tiny fellow, no more than a quarter of an inch in diameter from tip to tip. After a while it became clear that he was not constructing a web. He was weaving something small and tightly-bound. All this sea-going had taught him a thing or two: it looked at first like a kind of hammock. As the structure took shape and he settled into the heart of it and continued to wind filaments around his own body I realised what he was up to: he was building his own death-bed, driven on by a final genetic impulse. The spider had somehow survived life on the deck of *Mingming II* for two and a half weeks. He had built several webs, one with a diameter of several feet, under the most difficult conditions. The webs had been washed away, but somehow he had remained on board. He had made the long journey forward, looking for the right niche for the building of his final structure. Now, in the sheltered corner of the window, where he could attach his threads close together, he was using the last of his energy and the last of his silk-making resources to create a cocoon in which he could curl up and die. It was a quietly elegant statement. He knew that his position was hopeless; that his time was up. Somehow aware that a web was now of no avail, he had set about building his own mausoleum. There was a lesson to be drawn from this acceptance of mortality, and from this creativity to the last, and from the appropriateness of this final act: the spider was somehow possessed of the will to die a proper spider's death.

Away from the boat, the cycle of life was shifting to a higher gear, for we were moving closer to shallower water, and to land. Some way astern a party of striped dolphins rehearsed their crazy acrobatics, throwing themselves skywards with mad twists and somersaults and landing any old how, often tail first. The first breeding birds appeared: flocks of kittiwakes heading intently south, and then Brünnich's guillemots in their ones and twos, whirring back the other way, bills laden with sand eels. The water around us took on a sepia hue as we crossed the two hundred metre contour. Bjørnøya was less than thirty-five miles ahead, and to celebrate this proximity a humpback whale raised its fluke just a few hundred yards off the starboard beam. For a second or two that massive agglomeration of V-shaped muscle, pale white and roughly edged with black, held its monumental pose, then slid down into the depths.

Humpback Whale fluking

14

I had been told that I was unlikely to see Bjørnøya; that during the summer months it is wrapped in a permanent blanket of fog and cloud. I had been told of a cruise ship captain who had passed close by for ten summers and never seen so much as a shoulder of rock. I tend to distrust what I am told, and was therefore a little dismayed, as we closed the island, to find that it was not merely wrapped in a blanket of fog and cloud, but that it was swaddled, submerged and suffocated under a contour-hugging shroud of such solidity that at first I thought it was the land itself. I even wrote *Landfall!* in the ship's log, convinced that one of the darker segments of this tight layering was not heavy moisture but the even heavier rock concealed beneath. As we closed the southern cape I realised that I had been fooled by my own optimism: there was not a jot of land to be seen. Fog, impenetrable and immutable, gripped the island.

By late evening we were scarcely moving; the wind had

snuck off, leaving us heaving in an easy swell. I lowered and lashed the sail, and made my dispositions. We were eight miles or so due south of the island. I was determined to see it, and so decided that once the breeze returned I would sail in as close as I dared, penetrating the fog until land was visible. If possible I would sail up the eastern side. Just as the latitudinal division between the Norwegian Sea and the Greenland Sea is indeterminate, so is the longitudinal border between these two seas and the Barents Sea to their east. Bjørnøya seemed to be a logical marker between the Greenland Sea and the Barents Sea; to sail up its eastern seaboard would mark, in all probability, our entry into the latter.

I slept in short bouts. By midnight the fog had extended out to envelop *Mingming II*. It was an uncompromising, cloying fog that made a mockery of my plan to sail in to within sight of the island. I turned in again and slept for another couple of hours.

There are precise moments in every voyage which are so clear and crystalline, so deeply impressive, that they become indelibly etched into the memory. At twenty minutes past two on the morning of Tuesday the twenty-second of July, after we had been at sea for seventeen and a half days, one such moment arrived. It was all the better for being totally unexpected. I stuck my head out of the hatch to check the state of the fog. *Oh!* The fog had gone. Ahead of us, brilliantly irradiated by the low-angled light of an Arctic early morning, the southern cliffs of Bjørnøya stood high and proud. Nothing more than a few trails of narrow cloud, mere wisps of moisture cutting horizontally across the rock and the green sward that topped it, marred the perfection of the scene. I could see the basic topography of the island laid out clearly: the tall southern cape; the higher peaks to the north-east; between the two a protrusion of low whalebacks that marked the island's sole anchorage; the lowlands trailing off to the north-west. The intensity of the light cut deep vertical striations of shadow into the cliffs. I was surprised at the richness of the grassy verdure that undulated above the ramparts; it was a lush, inviting green, suggestive of Alpine meadows and summer picnics. Patches of late-melting snow patterned the hollows. At one point the cliff-face had crumpled, tilting the green topping to a crazy and vertiginous angle that brought it almost down to sea level. At the southern extremity of the island a sharp tooth of rock rose to half the height of the cliffs behind, while it too had its outliers: a series of low and jagged razor-backs stretching to the south.

After an extended sea passage, almost any sort of land, seen from relatively close up, has a grainy, sculptural quality. It suggests a dimension absent from the flat planes of sea and sky, and re-introduces a broader palette of subtle colorations. If the land in question is a remote Arctic island, tall-cliffed and monumental, these effects reach an even greater intensity. Here was the form and pliable solidity of the earth's crust distilled to a single tableau of thrusting rock. It seemed to glow and shimmer. It was almost unreal, otherworldly, and perhaps it was; a reminder that we are slave to our perceptions, that what we see is not what necessarily is, but only what our senses interpret it to be. I sat in the hatchway and studied what I perceived to be an island, wondering how and why I found it so stirring, so beautiful. I tried to work out why I should respond in this way to one particular arrangement of molecules, but not to others. The conjoined seascape and landscape ahead was no more than an ephemeral combination of matter, enhanced by a particular source and intensity of light. Why was my response so deep-seated and visceral? Why should rock projecting from a cold sea evoke yearning, sadness, joy?

A little breeze came in from the west. I raised six panels of the sail and set us on a course that would bring us in to the east of Stappen, the southern headland. Bjørnøya, like all of the smaller islands of Svalbard, is a protected nature reserve. Closing the land, we fell in with a great bustle of breeding sea birds. Tight lines of Brünnich's guillemots criss-crossed the air. For the first time on this voyage squads of little auks raced here and there. A pear-shaped black guillemot traversed our stern. Adult guillemots, each accompanied by a diminutive chick scarcely beyond its fluffy stage, littered the surface in every direction. Their loud and throaty exclamations clogged the airwaves. Higher up, flocks of kittiwakes headed south on shallow wing beats.

It was a joyous explosion of life but it had its darker side. Just ahead, on our port bow, a great skua attacked a group of four guillemots: two adults and two chicks. The adults repelled borders with raucous squawking, lunging desperately at their aggressor. The skua retreated for a moment but then saw its chance. It flapped forward, grabbed a chick in its talons and flew off.

For a second or two I felt shocked at the raw brutality of what I had just seen. My reaction was no doubt amplified by the ugliness of the skua as against the innocent cuteness of its prey. Reason quickly prevailed. Guillemots eat fish; skuas eat guillemots. Such is the way of the world. The aesthetic appeal of the eater and the eaten is irrelevant; my anthropomorphic sentiments irrational.

Back at the scene, the adult guillemots lamented: *rrraow, rrroaw*. The chick, now aloft and suspecting that its day had started badly, and could yet get worse, issued its final words on the matter: *peep, peep*. The skua, breakfast assured, flew off in silence.

Bear Island from due south

15

The sea is more than water. It is more, too, than water heavy with mineral salts. Even were we to add in the billions of tons of microscopic organisms, the krill, the phytoplanktons and the like, that further enrich the ocean, we would still not arrive at a definition of the sea. The sea is the sum of its parts, and those parts include all of the life that subsists above and below its surface. A sea without fish and whales and sharks, without seals and turtles and crabs, is not a sea. Nor could a sea without petrels and shearwaters and albatrosses, without auks and gannets and terns and skuas, be considered a sea. The sea, above and below, is a living system. Like the land, it is defined as much by its fauna as by its composition.

Birds and sea mammals and chemistry provide a seamless liaison between the sea and the sky. Think of the great diving whales: the sperm whale for example. It is the air with which it fills its lungs which enables it to make its long and stupendous dives to unimaginable depths. Think of the great shearwater, which flies twenty thousand miles a year but can still dive to depths of sixty feet to find its food. Think of the killer whale, which can launch itself up beaches or onto ice floes to take its prey. At its margins the sea engages in a constant interchange, an interchange which extends to gases and chemicals and heat and cold. The sea is a living system, but it is not hermetically sealed.

The sea seems broad, powerful, timeless, and therefore invulnerable. For millions of years it supported a thriving mass of life. Its shores were tumultuous with herds of seals and sea-lions and walruses; its sea-side cliffs were dense with the birds that lived off its bounty; its depths were home to whale numbers we can now only dream of, to shoaling fish in their trillions. It was a rich, pulsating, dynamic expression of the vital force.

I knew, as we neared the south cape of Bjørnøya, that what I was seeing was a pale parody of how things used to be. The life of the sea was making a show of health and prosperity, but it lacked conviction. Bjørnøya had not yet attained the forlorn and desolate state of its more southern counterparts like Foula, but I sensed that this was only a matter of time. Ultimately there could be no protection from the contagions of over-fishing, pollution, acidification and warming.

For millions of years the sea has maintained itself in a self-regulated equilibrium. Now it is stressed beyond redemption. That the poisons and imbalances should come from an outside, terrestrial agency only adds to the poignancy of the oceans' demise.

High above, another great skua was at work, harassing a flock of screaming, mewing kittiwakes. Below, we passed a puffin dead in the water, its legs a bright, almost phosphorescent red; two stiff trails of blood.

Tea Island from east (Southern Half)

16

We closed the land and the wind freshened, then dropped, then freshened again. Here the junk rig was at its best: it took only a few seconds to readjust the sail to the prevailing wind strength. As we approached the lee of the high cliffs, several miles offshore, great thudding gusts came down, forcing an instantaneous reduction of sail from six panels to two. A few minutes later I was raising sail again. Thus is the wind in the Arctic: unstable, capricious.

I studied the form and the colours of the eastern cliffs, well-lit by the morning sun. The grass-topped slopes of the southern headland soon gave way to bare rock, its predominantly pink coloration moderated by a sheen of grey lichen. As we progressed north the rock dropped away to form a low saddle, and took on a more rounded, barren aspect. The grass that crowned the southern cliffs was evidently the last expression of something homely and temperate: from here on we would see nothing but naked stone. We passed by the low razorbacks of Måkehl, the small island that shelters the island's only anchorage. I peered in as best I could but could see no sign of any vessel. A few minutes later a pelagic fishing boat, distinctly Nordic in form, appeared on the northern horizon. I watched it closely for a while, wondering whether it was working, and whether I would be forced to take some sort of evasive action. It was steaming steadily south, though, a mile or two to seaward of us, and so quickly passed and was gone. We lost the sunlight, too, as two layerings of cloud, one high and scaly, the other low and ragged, formed themselves out of nothing to rob the day of its early morning sparkle. The waist of low rock fell away almost to sea level before launching itself skywards to create the island's most impressive feature: the great buttresses of the Miseryfjellet. I could only conjecture as to the origins of this awkward Anglo-Nordic name: Misery Mountains. I found them grandiose rather than miserable. They rose from the sea with steeply-sloped scree topped by a rampart of vertical cliffs. The horizontal sedimentary layering of these cliffs was offset by their pattern of vertical gullies and indentations, themselves somewhat at odds with the splayed slopes beneath. Nor did the mountains reach their pinnacle at the cliff-tops. Above, the rock reverted to great rounded domes that reached their maximum height some miles inshore. The smoothness of these hills was clearly the work of an ice-cap and sure enough, at the mid-point of the range, the domes and the cliffs and the lower slopes were furrowed out, by a now-defunct glacier, into a giant half-pipe that led from the summit right down to the water's edge. There was much that was humbling in the scale and symmetry of this sculpting, and in the forces and the time required to accomplish it. These mountains, reposing in silence above the Barents Sea, combined grandeur and solitude and a seeming timelessness.

The brief appearance of the fishing boat had marred our

arrival at Bjørnøya. I knew it was unreasonable to expect to have these far-flung places entirely to myself; there was always the chance of meeting a cruise ship or a fishing boat. Our planet is small and crowded, and even eleven hundred miles of sailing to the Far North gave no guarantee of a few hours' respite from the commercial and the humdrum. I knew well enough too that although I regularly practised the conceit of trying to see these places through the eyes of the early discoverers, and liked to think that I was 'exploring' the Arctic, there was in reality nothing left, in the physical sense, to explore. The only legitimate exploration I was engaged in was that of my own psyche.

That particular fellow, prone to a hundred weaknesses, received another jolt from the unexpected appearance, astern and well inshore, of a sail. A sail! It was outrageous! Another yacht, in what I already considered to be my exclusive territory! What a damn cheek! What was going on here? Was the Barents Sea becoming a northern version of the Solent? The vessel had clearly snuck out from the anchorage, and was now advancing rapidly north, tight in to the edges of the Miseryfjellet. I watched it glumly as it gradually overhauled us, a tiny triangle of white against the darkening backdrop. After a long internal debate I assembled my little hand-held VHF radio and announced our presence to a silent world: *This is yacht Mingming II, yacht Mingming II blah blah blah...*

For the next hour or so I sent out a regular call to the interloper, but no reply came. I was not surprised: *Mingming II*, low and grey and furtive, had probably not been spotted. It was better thus; better to ignore each other and let those aboard get on with their own idea of an adventure.

The northern end of the Miseryfjellet fell away almost sheer to the lowlands that constitute most of the island. These now stretched away northwards in a featureless black line only a few feet above sea level. An examination of the chart showed that this low plateau of rock is indented with thousands of small lakes, and that the bottoms of these lakes are often below sea level. I pictured the whole thing in cross-section: rock somehow scooped out and corrugated; rain and melt-water held in basins deeper than the line of the sea. It was hard to reconcile this landscape with the adjacent explosion of mountain to the south-east, hard to imagine how two such contrasting geological processes had managed to operate side by side. There was something forlorn about these northern flatlands; an appropriate impression, given that Björnøya's outline resembles nothing more than a giant and inverted tear-drop.

Little auks clearly preferred this flat coastland: they had by now displaced Brünnich's guillemots as the predominant species of auk. Inevitably, too, a black guillemot or two flew past. Over the years I have learned that wherever little auks congregate, there are likely to be a few black guillemots. There is some affinity in their preferred habitat, but not in the scale of their reproduction. I have only ever seen black guillemots in ones and twos, never in big flocks. I tried to work out why this was, why they never seem to proliferate. Do they have a more refined or obscure diet? Are a pot belly and bright red legs a hindrance to courtship and mating? Are they less adept at parenting? Are they not aggressive enough to deter predators or establish breeding grounds? Are their eggs the wrong shape? Are they innately antisocial? I long one day to see the flight of an extravagant and joyous flock of black guillemots. What a fine sight that would be as they all whirred along, ebony bombshells, white-flecked wings a-blur, bellies sagging, crimson legs trailing, improbably air-borne.

The cloud closed in further and the rain started. The mood of the island had changed completely since the early sun had caught it in a flood of light. Top-of-the-morning brilliance had given way to midday brooding. The island was rapidly reverting to its bound-up, hidden state.

Midday came. We had somehow covered seventy miles since the last noon position; evidence of a strong north-going current hereabouts.

Our course was now to the north-east, and so we were pulling away from the last thin wedge of coastline. Through the thickening gloom I could just make out the pale dot of the other yacht's mainsail. It was still hugging the coast, no doubt bound for the west coast of Spitsbergen and Longyearben, its capital. I was glad that our route lay elsewhere, that we were heading for the places where sailors rarely go. As the two yachts diverged I felt that now our voyage was really starting, that I would soon grasp its essence. Thus far we had followed well-worn paths; from here on it was up to me to create a worthwhile track through the less-travelled wastes which lay ahead.

Within an hour or so a thick fog rolled in, reinforced by driving rain. For the first time on this voyage I felt cold, and so brewed up a mug of hot bouillon. The wind swung around from west to south and back to south-west, where it finally settled with a vengeance. Bjørnøya was long since gone, lost in the massing moisture astern. Driven on by a building sea, with just a panel or two of sail set, *Mingming II* bent to her task. I broke out my favourite pink blanket to add some weight to my sleeping bag and thus well-swaddled slept on and off, dreaming of black cliffs and ice floes and warm embraces.

Black Guillemot

17

The world was reduced once again to nothing more than a tight sphere of grey sea and grey fog. I knew that it would be easy to develop a loathing for this veil which, for so many days of this voyage, had obscured the sun, the sky and the smooth line of the horizon. Yes, it would be easy to rail against this constant murk that weighed down, suffocating the world. There is nothing to be gained, however, by complaint. I repeated my guiding mantra: *don't hope; don't expect; don't complain,* and looked out at the swirling fog with indifference.

Thinking about it a little more, I realised that far from being something adverse and hateful, this endless fog was a boon to the voyage. It sharpened my seamanship; it forced me to be more alert; it reinforced the notion that at sea unseen perils are always lurking. If the fog made me feel ill at ease and on edge, then that was a good thing. Fair winds and clear horizons breed complacency; this fog was a good antidote to any laxness.

It went much further than that, though. This fog was a stimulant to my imagination. With nothing to see I had to create my own picture of what lay beyond the grey blanket that bound us; I was forced to conjure up my own seascape. Here now was the curve of a far horizon, its line broken only by the topsails of an ancient whale-ship ghosting north. Over there uncharted islands rose from the sea, an archipelago of black cliff. Astern, just out of view, a Kraken-like monster tracked us, its eyes glaucous and sad. The fog left me free to create whatever I liked. There was nothing wrong, moreover, with its coldness and its clamminess. What could be more appropriate and more character-building for a sailor heading to the Arctic wastes? On that score, this fog was to be welcomed, perhaps even celebrated.

Thinking more positively about it, I uncovered the metaphors hitherto hidden beneath my own prejudice. The fog that obscured what lay around us day after day was surely truer to our progress across the unfathomable ocean of life than the hard clarity of an unblemished horizon. We may think we see everything in perfect focus, just as it is, and thus feel comforted and reassured, but is this not a gross illusion? Are we not all stumbling along through a fog of misunderstanding, willingly complicit in our self-delusion? This fog that gripped us was closer to the reality of things; more expressive of their impenetrable mystery. I had lived a whole lifetime in a kind of foggy incomprehension; nothing was any clearer than it had ever been. I was no nearer understanding what I was doing on this sphere hurtling through space; where my flesh came from, or the mind that went with it, or the energy that propelled a hundred billion galaxies through unimaginable time and distance.

I had never fully grasped, either, the more mundane question of what impelled me out onto this wild and frigid sea. Oh, I could rationalise it alright, one way and another, but this was not to get to the true heart of the matter. For sure, it was one of a million ways to fill the hours between birth and death, and was no better and no worse, and certainly no more meaningful, than sitting on a sofa watching day-time television, or taking classes in line-dancing, or stealing old ladies' handbags. We all have to do *something*. Sailing around the ocean serves no moral purpose, and one would be hard-pressed to ascribe to it any form of utility; a large part of my life had been devoted to perfecting an intrinsically useless activity.

To be thus sailing along, blindfolded by the persistent fog, was therefore revelatory. I could see my own blindness. I could also start to see the latent beauty of this suffocating pall. There was nothing more honest than this obscurity, and in a world overlaid by deceit of one sort or another, nothing was more beautiful than its uncompromised honesty.

With Bjørnøya now well astern we raced to the northeast through the fog and rain. Yes, the weather was honest, and it was foul, and despite its illuminating features, I grew apprehensive. It was all very well to learn to love the truthfulness of a thick fog, but what if we were sailing willy-nilly into a sea littered with ice floes? I had no idea whether or not there may be stray sea ice close ahead. It was unlikely, but it could not be ruled out. The seas, too, were becoming steeper as we neared the shallow waters of the Spitsbergen Banks. To sail blithely on into possible danger, with a strong following wind, a rough sea and zero visibility, was not an acceptable strategy. I had no seamanlike option but to cede to the conditions. I reduced sail to a single panel, and put *Mingming II* into a kind of hove-to mode, gently fore-reaching more or less beam on to the wind and seas. Thus hunkered down, we could bide our time and wait for a better day to continue our progress north.

Hopen ~ first view from the south

18

We crossed the Spitsbergen Banks, in depths as niggardly as those of the North Sea, with a halting, oblique track. For three days we ranged gently north-east, sometimes on port tack, sometimes on starboard. My priority, apart from defusing the danger of the howling south-westerly and its relentless fog, was to line us up for an accurate landfall at the south cape of Hopen. It would have been easy, in these conditions, to miss the island altogether, to run rapidly through the fifty-mile wide channel that separates Hopen from the string of tiny islands to the west. Hopen is scarcely more than a mile wide on its east-west axis; my approach therefore had to be accurate.

For the first time, I studied the features of the island carefully on the chart. Thus far I had conceived of it as nothing more than a long, low worm of an island, devoid of much interest apart from its general improbability. Looking more closely, I was startled to find that this initial and somewhat lazy assessment was wide of the mark. It was a worm, for sure, eighteen miles long and not much more than a mile wide, but there the comparison ended. Along most of its length, the island rose to a height of a thousand feet or so. It was an imposing monolith, by any standards. The chart gave no detail on the contours of the island, so I had no idea whether its central ridge was a long razorback, or whether the rock rose cliff-like from the sea, creating a flat-topped topography. The more I looked at the chart, the more determined I was to find a way in close. Here was an extraordinary and virtually unknown island. Even now it spends a good part of each year locked into the pack-ice. I wanted to examine it and to feel its atmosphere, to see how well it accorded with the bleak and barren Barents Sea that surrounded it.

By midnight on Thursday the twenty-fourth of July, our twentieth day at sea, I had manoeuvred *Mingming II* into a position twenty miles or so upwind of Hopen from which we could launch our final approach to the island. With just one panel of sail set in a wind that was blowing as fiercely as ever, I set a definitive course to bring us in marginally to the east of Kapp Thor, Hopen's southern cape. I was not hopeful of being able to see much of the island, but if I could approach within a mile or two the chances would be improved.

For more than ten days we had been sailing in predominantly poor visibility. We were now approaching 76°North, and since our crossing of the Arctic Circle, six hundred miles or so astern, had seen little but fog. I had learned to love this fog, or at any rate to accept it without rancour, and had banished all hope and expectation of anything other than this permanent pall. I was therefore surprised, as I kept a keen watch on the northern horizon, to detect a hint of a lightening of the sky away to the north-east. A sliver of silver soon became a sliver of washed-out blue. The sliver widened and the blue deepened. There was soon no doubt about it: the back end of the weather system that had smothered us for so long was moving rapidly south.

The change came with unerring rapidity. One moment we were in fog and rain and a freezing wind; within the hour the sky had cleared to a blazing cocktail of azure leavened by the shallow-angled and piercing early morning sunlight. This sudden blinding clarity was almost shocking. The line of the horizon was now inscribed with draughtsman-like precision against the blue beyond; the white caps of the still-ragged sea shone and sparkled; the ocean itself turned a deep indigo; *Mingming II*'s deck and mast and sail glowed in a flood of hard-edged light. I had grown unused to such lucidity. I mistrusted it, but welcomed it nonetheless. It was a kind of liberation, albeit a false one. Now I could pretend once more that all was well with the world. A clear sky and an unconstrained sun can quickly banish doubt; they force one back into the immediacy of time and place. They seduce with their surface glitter. They murmur sweet nothings into a receptive ear: *Don't you bother your head, old son. Just relax and enjoy yourself.*

This swift change in fortune was more than a mere meteorological merry-go-round. It marked our passage into the Arctic High, the system of elevated pressure that dominates the summer weather in these high latitudes, and so signalled our arrival at the Far North. It was the second major transition of the voyage. From here on we were unlikely to have much in the way of dirty weather or strong winds. After three weeks at sea *Mingming II* was now in the conditions for which she had primarily been designed.

With maximum visibility now restored it took only a quick scan of the northern horizon to locate Kapp Thor, a soft-angled mitre topped by a single halo of wispy cloud. With the breeze falling away I raised a couple of panels of the sail and headed straight for it.

It took just seven hours of gentle sailing to bring *Mingming II* as close as I dared to the base of Kapp Thor. With a more reliable wind I may have snuck in closer, but by eleven in the morning we were becalmed two miles off; close enough to examine the extraordinary geological detailing of this prodigious headland, far enough off to give a margin of safety. We were now unequivocally into a remote corner of the Arctic, and I had to be careful. The waters here, especially up the west side of the island, are shallow. Already I could see a line of ice floes grounded at the south-west foot of the cape. A single lump of ice, it too seemingly aground, lay directly between us and the cape's southern face. With the wind gone for a while I checked our drift. We seemed to be heading east-south-east, away from the land, and so I felt a little easier.

Kapp Thor, and the long, almost straight line of mountain behind that was now coming into view as we edged to the east, was an impressive sight. The cape thrust skywards like a massive four-sided pyramid. All it lacked was an apex: its peak had been sliced off at a shallow angle. Its sedimentary striations combined regularity of line with an almost faultlessly horizontal orientation. There was no sense here of rock forced one way or the other, no echoes of tectonic grinding. This horizontal regularity did not mean that each face of the cape was smooth. Some working of wind or water or perhaps ice had carved out shallow vertical declivities that gave each cliff a corrugated look. Once again, though, these vertical corrugations were almost perfectly matched in form and placement. A billion tons of compressed rock had somehow been sculpted over time with extraordinary precision. It was this harmony and regularity of form that was most striking, for the same characteristics stretched along the whole eighteen miles of the island.

There was more to it than that, though. As I came to know the island better, becalmed as I was to its south and east, and later to its west, I began to understand that this almost perfect patterning is not confined simply to the fine detail of the island's geology, but to its overall topography as well. The island is not laid out along its principal axis as one continuous slug of rock. It is in fact a series of slugs, each joined to the next by a low and narrow valley. From a distance, when viewed either from the east or the west, the island is nothing more than a string of six gargantuan half-submerged sausages, or, if you prefer a more muscular metaphor, a line of giant railway carriages. Each slug, or sausage, or railway carriage, is of almost the same height and length and overall configuration as the next. Each of these six components is about three miles long and a thousand feet high. Within this general scheme there are some minor variations: Kapp Thor, or more precisely the peak directly behind it, the Iversenfjellet, achieves a little more height than the rest, and the valley to the immediate north of the Iversenfjellet is somewhat wider and lower than all the others.

I took advantage of the calm to exit the hatch and put an extra lashing on the three mainsheet blocks where they were attached to the after rail. One of the fittings was looking vulnerable. Later I also replaced some frayed line at the aft end of the top batten. After three weeks at sea these were the only precautionary repairs I had to make to keep the rig in good working order.

With the sail bundle lashed firmly to the boom gallows I sat in the hatchway and watched the evolution of light, shadow and cloud-cover over the island. In the high Arctic, cloud and mist can form and un-form in just a few seconds, in particular in proximity to land. These provisional clouds take on shapes and dimensions unknown further south. I watched a demonstration of the most impressive formation of all: colossal cigar-shaped clouds that stretch from one horizon to the other. These huge Zeppellins, fuzzy-edged and dark-hearted, appear in moments out of thin air. Their symmetry is exquisite. Sometimes they can deliver a hatful of wind, sometimes none at all. I decided they needed their own classification, and so dubbed them *Hindenbergus arcticus*, for they parade across the skies with all the inflated grandeur of a doomed dirigible.

I was struck, as I watched the constant interplay of light and moisture over the island, by the repetitive timelessness of the process. This kaleidoscopic evolution had gone on every day, at this very spot, and against this same backdrop of sea and ice and crust, for perhaps a hundred million years. Our few hours there constituted just one single day in more than thirty-six billion days. Perhaps it was the remoteness, and the overwhelming muteness of the rock, that brought home the weight of all those days and all those evolutions. For a fleeting moment I sensed the mind-numbing dimensions of geological time, and heard the echoes of its silence.

Horizon to East under low Cloud.

19

We lay there for a day or so, *Mingming II* and I, by now comfortable companions of the road, and grew easy too with our presence at Hopen. It was so much more than I had ever imagined, so much greater in scale and effect. The cloud and mist came and went, but as at Bjørnøya, the general trend was a gradual thickening. By the following morning, as we worked our way to the north-east in a tiny stuttering breeze that had come up from the east, all but the bottom few hundred feet of the island's rock was firmly locked into a solid layer of stratus. This cloud had drawn the life out of the prevailing light, and so turned the rock it topped into a frieze of unmitigated black. I made a sketch of it in the ship's log: thickly hatched cloud lowering over a band of black ink. I could not find a way to reproduce the five tiny points of intense light that pierced the declivities between each portion of the island. In the flesh they glowed, but no amount of contrasting with pen and ink could capture the organic brightness of the original.

I sketched a flight of Brünnich's guillemots too, and once again could find no way to transmit the blinding whiteness of their under parts. The air hereabouts was buzzing with birds. Every guillemot was an exact replica, in size and plumage, of every other guillemot, whether male or female. I wondered how it would be if this level of identicalness had persisted in the human race. I tried to imagine a society in which everyone, man or woman, looked exactly the same; a world, for example, in which five billion humans all looked exactly like Prince Charles, or Karl Marx, or Marilyn Monroe: wife, husband, daughter, boss, bank manager, mistress; a society in which there was a perfect physical resemblance between rugby players and ballet dancers, prostitutes and philosophers.

Moving beyond the frivolous, I wondered whether human differentiation, probably the greatest of any species, is a cause of that species' undoing. Is man over-attached to his individuality? Does it lead to the wrong kind of competition? Is there something inherently destructive in our need to assert our differences over others? Human society seemed a fragile, fractious construct compared to the undeviating collective endeavour of the flocks of guillemots working to and fro past *Mingming II*. I watched carefully the groups heading back to the nesting grounds. Each flock demonstrated a range of success in finding food. Some birds were empty-billed, some carried a sand eel or two, yet there was no attempt by the less successful to steal food from the more successful. There was something edifying in each bird's calm acceptance of the order of things. Each bird simply got on with what it had to do, without complaint, regret, blame, or rancour. It was beautiful to watch, this incessant passage of hard-working creatures untainted by murderous intent, uncontaminated by irrational delusion, unsullied by greed.

With the faintest of zephyrs now occasionally ruffling the sea from the east, it would have been possible for us to sail in close to the eastern seaboard of the island. It was a tempting proposition, but one I resisted. Caution and good seamanship required that I keep a good offing, especially in such an inconsistent onshore wind. A well-developed aversion to lee shores, combined with a dislike of being becalmed close to land, were more than enough to persuade me to stay hard on what wind there was, moving gently north-east parallel with the coast. I needed a good margin to be sure of weathering the northern end of the island and avoiding an awkward trap.

It was only later that I discovered that Hopen is home to polar bears and to several men and women. In summer the bears move north with the ice, but the men and women remain. There are four of them and they maintain the Hopen meteorological radio station. I had seen Hopen Radio marked on the chart, and assumed that it was some kind of unmanned signal. Three huts are located on the eastern side of the island, about four miles north of Kapp Thor, in the valley just north of Hopen's second highest peak, the Werenskioldfjellet.

On balance I am glad that I was not aware of this last pocket of human habitation on our route north. Without that knowledge I was still able to think of the island as pure wilderness and to appreciate it as such. Nor was I tempted to do anything silly: to sail in close to try to locate the settlement, for example.

As it was, I maintained my sangfroid, and stayed well offshore, and considered instead our trajectory once Hopen had been cleared. The grounded ice floes around Kapp Thor suggested that from here on there was every possibility of heavier concentrations of ice. We were now little more than sixty miles from the huge ice-cap on the island of Edgeøya, and its calving glacier, the Stonebreen, away to the north-north-west. As my first priority was to make as much northing as possible, it seemed sensible to keep well clear of Edgeøya. I decided to maintain a course to the north-east that would bring us to the islands of Kong Karls Land. If it were feasible, I could then carry on to Kvitøya, bringing *Mingming II* to 80°North. If at any point I decided to turn back, I would head south-west towards Edgeøya with a view to examining the ice-cap and its glacier. This plan gave me the best of both worlds: a strong challenge, but plenty of compensation if that challenge proved impossible.

Brünnich's Guillemots

20

Even a hard-bitten sailor has his fantasies. Even though there are limits to the possible, because, for example, it is not possible for any yacht to penetrate solid pack-ice, this does not preclude dreams of the near-impossible. And what is adventure if not a re-examination of what is possible?

For many months, since the arrival at home one day of my Norwegian chart for the Barents Sea, I had harboured a near-impossible fantasy. It was a fantasy so personal and so outrageous that so far, in the writing of this account, I have had neither the desire nor the courage to mention it. Now I realise that such an omission is unacceptable, from the point of view both of honesty and of completeness. I have already said that to a large extent these voyages to the northern wastes are as much an exploration of one man's psyche as an exploration of physical space. It is appropriate, therefore, that even the most hidden recesses of that psyche are revealed.

My secret obsession was triggered by the discovery that

hidden away in these northern waters there is another clearly defined sea. Few have heard of it, and I am sure that few could, with confidence, point out its exact location on an appropriate chart. There is no shame in not having heard of this sea. I was in my sixty-seventh year when I found it, and I could well have missed it. Only a passing knowledge of Norwegian nautical terms, acquired from many years of using Norwegian charts, stopped me from overlooking its existence.

The Norwegians, who know a thing or two about remote waters, call a sea a *havet*. The Arctic Ocean, for example, is the *Polhavet*, the Barents Sea is the *Barentshavet*, and so on. Whenever I see the five letters *havet* appended to a name, my attention sharpens, for I am, in a lowly way, a collector of seas. An ornithologist lists the birds he has seen; a Don Juan lists the women he has seduced; I list the seas in which I have sailed. In the sister yachts *Mingming* and *Mingming II* I had, when I discovered the existence of this new sea, sailed in five seas. They are: the Celtic Sea, the North Sea, the Norwegian Sea, the Greenland Sea and the Labrador Sea. To these could now be added the Barents Sea: six in all. We had sailed in the Atlantic Ocean, of course, but an ocean is too big, too loose, to be of interest to a collector of seas. It is the tightness and specificity of a sea that lends it its piquancy. The discovery of a seventh sea, the Victoria Sea, whose existence is so unlikely and whose location is so improbable, triggered an immediate passion: one day to sail in that sea.

To the east of the Svalbard group, and extending to even higher latitudes, lies the huge archipelago of islands, a hundred and ninety-one in all, known collectively as Franz Josef Land. The small patch of water that is the Victoria Sea or, as I first came to know it, the *Victoriahavet*, is located to the north of Franz Josef Land. Its name is linked to that of the westernmost island of the Franz Josef Land group, Victoria Island, named not directly for the long-dead queen, but for what was probably the first non-commercial vessel to penetrate these waters, the steam-yacht *Victoria*. The *Victoria* was owned by the English adventurer Arnold Pike, and was under the command of one Captain Nilsen when the island was sighted and named in 1898.

This brings us back to Kvitøya, the easternmost of the Svalbard group, and for which I was heading: Victoria Island lies just thirty-two nautical miles further east. By geography it is part of Svalbard, but the Russians laid claim to it in the thirties. Although Norway had previously exerted rights over the island, they did not contest the claim. It is now therefore part of Franz Josef Land.

The proximity of Kvitøya and Ostrov Victoriya – White Island and Victoria Island – raised some intriguing possibilities. Were we to penetrate as far as Kvitøya, the likelihood was that the waters on the eastern side would be less ice-infested. However, allowing for twelve miles of territorial water for each of Kvitøya and Victoria Island, there is a band of international water just eight miles wide between the two. What a mouth-watering proposition that would be: to slip between Svalbard and Franz Josef Land in such a narrow channel of unclaimed ocean! There was something else too. If, whilst heading either north or south, we passed to the east of Victoria Island, that would put us definitively into Franz Josef Land. That too was a happy prospect.

It would not, however, put us into the Victoria Sea, for that lies away to the north-east, to the north of the main group of Franz Josef Land islands. To sail to the Victoria Sea would require the withdrawal of the summer pack-ice thereabouts to well above 83°North. This had happened in both the two previous years, but was by no means guaranteed: the polar ice areas move inconsistently.

The other requirement was a level of resolve which I am not sure I possess, and this was the nexus that interested me.

Where exactly is the point at which desire is overcome by discouragement? What is the basis for blind will, the need to push on regardless? Is there a moment when rational endeavour transgresses to the irrational? And in any case, can anything we do be defined as either rational or irrational? Rationality presupposes some kind of objective, external measure, a yardstick based on pure reason. The tool of reason is logic, but I was unsure as to how logic could be applied to this kind of enterprise.

What I did know is that there is a fine line between over-stretching and not going far enough. I also knew that in general I am not inclined to over-stretching; my preference is for gentle, orderly and relaxed sailing. It is impossible to feel relaxed when sailing a small engineless yacht too close to ice, and so on balance I prefer an honourable retreat over unseemly heroics.

For the whole of the voyage so far the more opaque areas of my mind had been ranging further to the north-east, and wondering whether I might make a bid to sail to the Victoria Sea. As usual, I had no definite plan or intention. It did not look as if the ice was going to recede as much as in the two previous years, so getting that far was an unlikely prospect anyway. Then there was the question of will. I had no idea, as we left Hopen astern, how long the desire to keep on north would hold. I was wholly at the mercy of two disparate elements: sea-ice and my own resolve.

Seal   ← Relative Sizes →   Walrus

21

The breeze stuttered its way round to the south-west, and soon Hopen, a narrowing streak of black sandwiched between sea and sky, thinned to nothing. With the wind on the port quarter we rolled gently north. The softness of the weather, and the easy calmness of our progress, underlined our arrival deep into the summer Arctic. With two hundred miles or so to sail to reach our next target, the islands of Kong Karls Land, I settled back to the routines of passage-making, with one exception: from here on I would heave-to to sleep. This was an obvious and necessary precaution, given that we were now less than fifty miles south-east of the ice-cliffs of Edgeøya and approaching 77°North.

Hopen had been something of an unexpected and grandiose revelation, and I was still reflecting on everything I had seen and felt. With the island now twelve miles astern and lost to view, I had no expectation that it had yet more to offer, but I was wrong. A loud and breathy *hrrrmph!*

which immediately brought to mind the exhalations of our old friend the Cuvier's Beaked Whale, encountered some years earlier in the Bay of Biscay, exploded close by. Within a second or two I located the slick of a creature which had surfaced and dived, just off the port quarter. A moment later a massive brown head appeared just a few yards to port. I had just enough time to take in its unmistakable features – two big, round and lugubrious eyes, two sizeable and strikingly yellow tusks, one scrunched-up nose – before it dived again. A walrus! I had never seen one before, but a walrus falls into that class of objects, like the Eiffel Tower or an Elvis Presley impersonator, that you recognise wholly and immediately on first sight.

It was unexpected on two counts. Firstly that of latitude: I had thought that I would have to be to the north of Svalbard to encounter walruses. Secondly my expectation was that walruses are only seen close to land and the beaches on which they haul out. It took only a moment's reflection to realise what a daft idea that was. Walrus colonies can reach huge numbers. Walruses are big animals that need considerable nourishment; they must of necessity range far and wide to hunt.

Another head broached the surface further off to port, then another. Within half a minute it had become clear that there was a herd of nine or ten animals ranged around us. We had clearly piqued their curiosity: every head that poked up examined us for a few seconds then disappeared. Several aspects of the walruses surprised me. Their heads and bull necks were huge, probably seven or eight times bigger than a seal's head. More striking than this was their colour. The big creatures of the sea generally come in a palette of blues, blacks, greys and silvers; cold, sleek colours that somehow imply speed and steely efficiency. The walruses were of a homely light brown somehow at odds with the frigid ocean in which they were swimming. Their faces too were comical rather than menacing: startled, moustached, bespectacled and buck-toothed, they looked like a pack of kindly but half-witted uncles up from the country in their brown tweed suits.

On seeing the walruses I immediately dropped the sail down to a couple of panels and let the mainsheet go. Thus lying a-hull I did my best to film and photograph them. As is so often the case with sea mammals, it was an almost impossible task. By the time I had homed in on a head it had already disappeared. Most of the animals kept a good distance from the boat, reducing the chances of good images.

Whenever I meet something worth recording I have to make an immediate decision: do I film or do I photograph? Wildlife encounters are often fleeting. There are just a few seconds available in which to capture something of the moment, with only rarely the luxury of enough time to take both still and moving images. Each option has its advantages and disadvantages. Stills are of much higher quality and can be enlarged and improved. They can be framed more accurately using a proper viewfinder. On the other hand they can lack the immediacy and power, and of course the sounds, of a film clip. A small hand-held camcorder, with a screen for a viewfinder, is fiendishly difficult to point accurately, from a moving yacht, at a moving target. In most conditions it is almost impossible to see what is on the screen; it is more often than not just a case of pointing the camera in the direction of the object and hoping. Despite this, there is nothing to equal even a mediocre series of moving images for capturing the essence and excitement of a wildlife encounter, particularly with the larger sea mammals.

Whether using a camera or a camcorder, and whether conditions are favourable to photography or not, I have a general rule, which is always to record the moment. An imperfect record is better than no record, and the assumption that a better moment will present itself later is usually false. I therefore recorded the encounter with the walruses, but not well, and in retrospect I know I ought to have spent a lot more time working at it. However, I mistakenly thought that I would soon have other opportunities to capture walruses on film. Having met them so easily much further south than anticipated, I assumed that from here on I would see them regularly. Frustrated by my lack of success, and by the poor light for photography, I decided to abandon the attempt and try again at the next encounter. I raised sail again and carried on north.

I really should have known better. How I regret that lazy capitulation. How I wish I were back there again and able to rerun the scene. What efforts I would make if I could have that time again. Yes, it was a stupid and careless decision, to try again another day. I am still waiting for that day. These were the first walruses sighted on this voyage, but also the last. During the weeks that followed I searched in vain for more of those big brown heads and rheumy eyes, but the bounty of the sea is limited. I sailed on north, too hastily, and may never see a walrus again.

Minke Whale ~ Second Phase in Surfacing Sequence.

22

With Hopen well astern and the southern end of the huge
island of Edgeøya, a true island of the ice that will have a
major role to play in this narrative, now to our west, we were
unequivocally into the north-west sector of the Barents Sea.
This was the playground we had been heading for, and so I
felt that we had arrived. I was therefore in no hurry. As long
as we proceeded carefully, and paid infinite attention to every
detail, there was without doubt many a surprise and many a
reward to come.

   It is only by making the voyage that one can discover
its true rationale; and that rationale is almost without fail
something quite different from what was expected. Every
voyage will have its defining motif, but that motif, whatever
it may be, will become evident in its own time and in its own
way; it cannot be imposed. That is why each voyage is a totally
fresh adventure. The idea of the voyage, its outline structure,
is no more than a loose framework in which the unforeseen

is given free range. The pleasure lies in this discovery of the unforeseen, in creating the possibilities for the unlikely, the outlandish and, sometimes, the sublime. A good voyage must be meticulously prepared for, but not over-planned. It must be allowed its own space in which to develop. The true and well-made voyage is a process of creation; action moulded to form.

I was still waiting for this voyage to reveal its particular sense. I had not yet determined its central thread, but that was a good thing. It meant that the voyage was still alive and fizzing with possibility. I sensed that we were probably now close to its defining moments, but what those would be I had not the slightest idea.

Despite the increasing chill of a soft and gyrating wind, I therefore felt warm inside, and supremely relaxed. Three years' thought and hard physical labour had brought us to this one point in space and time. All that work, and all the odd-ball ideas infused into *Mingming II,* had translated themselves into our easy presence in this raw wilderness. The fact that we were now here absolved and justified the near-insanity of the effort that lay behind it.

The breeze came and went, and with it swathes of gossamer mist. This was a wholly different fog from its southern cousins; there was something almost apologetic and hesitant about it. It was scarcely more than a thickening of the air, enough to obscure the horizon, but not enough to defuse the gentle rays of the Arctic sun. From time to time I had no choice but to lower and lash the sail, leaving us to drift through this opaque but glowing blanket of moisture. A calm always brought with it a minke whale nosing its way in great circles around us, and overlaying the creak and groan of our roll with its intermittent exhalations. It brought fulmars too, now in their hundreds, dozing peaceably all around the boat.

The sea slowly eased off and flattened, so that sometimes, lying there in a now immaculate calm, the dense calm of a deep-hewn sepulchre, I thought that I could hear the distant vibration of an engine. I could not attribute any rational cause to this murmuring, and so fancied that it must be the vibration of the universe, infinite matter pulsating in the grand silence. It is only now, as I write, and re-read my notes, and see the voyage in retrospect, that I realise that this distant growl was not imagined, that its cause was, in fact, the pulsating of matter; not general sidereal matter, but ice. What I was hearing was the ceaseless groaning of the Edgeøya ice-cap. I was soon to become familiar with the sounds of the ice-cap, but for the moment they were unknown to me, and so I had no choice but to conclude that my ears were picking up the hum of a hundred billion galaxies hard at work.

A little breeze came up from the east-north-east, bringing with it a patter of light rain, and setting us once more on our way. By midnight, or rather, by the final minutes of that particular division of an endless day, I needed to sleep for an hour or two, and so I reduced sail once more. We edged forward harmlessly while I slept. By three the next morning the cloud had lifted, freeing the horizon of mist and rain. With four panels set we got properly under way. At seven a large oval slick on the starboard bow signalled the arrival of another minke whale. The wind backed to north-north-east, heading us slightly west of north. I had as yet seen no indications of ice, and so was unperturbed at being set in towards the Olgastretet, or Olga Strait, the strip of water that separates the islands of Kong Karls Land from the larger islands to the west, Edgeøya and Barentsøya, and from the north-east headlands of Spitsbergen itself. By ten the wind was easing once more and we were back to six panels of the sail.

At just after eleven o'clock on the morning of Monday the twenty-eighth of July, our twenty-fifth day at sea, we made our landfall at Kong Karls Land. Several segments of land, one of them completely white, pushed above the horizon on the starboard bow. These were the higher peaks and plateaux of the group's principal island, Kongsøya. A few minutes later another line of black rock, interspersed with vertical strips of ice, appeared ahead: Svenskøya, the most westerly of the group. Our noon position gave a latitude of 78° 20.2'North.

The wind eased again and I slept for an hour. A light drizzle returned, not yet enough to obscure the land ahead. I raised all seven panels of the sail, and so in the faintest of breezes we were able to ghost smoothly on. The murmuring of the universe had long since gone. Our fulmar escort, too, had thinned to a token pair. In a silence broken only by the occasional hiss of water at the bow, we kept on north.

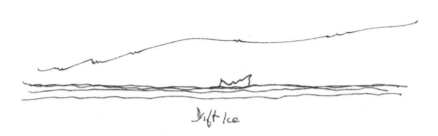

Drift Ice

23

The closest island was Svenskøya and for a while, with what wind there was, it looked as if we would be able to make a close approach. I could already make out the detailing of its tall cliffs topped by an almost perfectly level plateau. For some reason the eastern end of the island was bare of snow and ice, while the western side gleamed under an unbroken layer of white. A wide stretch of water, the Rivalensundet, separated Svenskøya from the less regular contours of Kongsøya to the east. In theory I had three options for navigating either through or round the islands. I could pass to the west of the entire group, via the Olgastretet; I could pass between Svenskøya and Kongsøya, using the Rivalensundet; or I could work our way round the eastern end of the group, passing to the east of the smallest of the main islands, Abeløya. My preference was for the last option. It was the safest choice, and would also ensure that I had a good look at Abeløya. This island was already puzzling me. It is not far from Kongsøya, just five miles or so, but I could see no sign of it. Everything we had seen so far was tall and imposing, and so I was expecting to see at least some hint of land in that direction. The horizon to the north-east of Kongsøya was unblemished.

A sailor can consider all of his options in the finest detail, but once the wind has gone he has no choice but to lower his sail and reflect on the joy of total immobility. The wind soon fell away completely, a layer of impenetrable mist rolled in, and so I lowered the sail and gave myself over to reflection. Once again we were marooned in a vaporous shroud. For a moment or two I had an urge to sing to the world and thus, perhaps, relieve the grey tension of the day, but I held my peace. It was better to listen and to watch; to absorb rather than emit. It would have been a kind of sacrilege, in any case, to have imposed frivolity on this imperturbable wasteland. My passage was ephemeral; it should be respectful too. I stood under the observation pod and watched and listened. In the heightened acoustic of this inverted box of bare wood I became conscious of the push and pull of my own breathing. My ears were drawn in to the sound of my breath passing in and out. It was alarming to realise how much depended on this involuntary pulmonary action. Everything depended on it, in fact. I checked the mechanics my own breathing; it was, after all, the continuing requirement for life. As soon as I started to think about it, the rhythm of my inhalations and exhalations became forced and irregular. Concentration and self-consciousness destroyed the natural flow. It was impossible to determine whether my breaths were shallower or deeper, or quicker or slower, than normal. There was a kind of paradox here: only by not thinking about it could I breathe naturally; and so I could never listen to the patterns of my involuntary breathing.

I tuned away from internal sound and absorbed the wholesome deathly silence of the world outside. Just once in a while that silence was profaned by the plaintive *rrraaoow!*

of a distant guillemot. Apart from that there was nothing. The day ground to a halt, devoid of all motion, all sound. I was not concerned. Time was no longer of the essence. Further north, the ice was getting on with its melting. Less ice meant more possibility.

The silver of the mist and the silver of the sea became fused and indecipherable; we were drowning in cold silver. I watched the softly pulsating surface of this silver sea and waited for the depths to yield up something huge and breathy and heart-stopping. Something would emerge from there, sooner or later. It always does. Sure enough, the head of a small seal rose for a second or two then disappeared. It was not much, and it was certainly not heart-stopping, but it was something.

The vapour thinned and thickened under a reluctant sun. Just once or twice the chequered slopes of Kongsøya showed themselves then were gone. Tiny zephyrs, nowhere near robust enough to induce a raising of the sail, caressed the sea this way and that with no logic to their direction or duration.

For twelve hours we lay there, our only motion a scarcely perceptible drift to the south-east. At five the next morning a hint of wind from the north-west persuaded me to raise all seven panels of the sail. It was not really a viable breeze, and I wrote in the ship's log that we were just playing at sailing. Mostly we just drifted; from time to time a close observation of the water alongside suggested we were moving forwards. The point of reference was the stream of surface detritus easing past: fulmar feathers from curls of down to discarded primaries; bits of seaweed, sometimes just a nodule or two, sometimes whole clumps; strange squiggles of white gunk; a square of blue plastic; tiny transparent slivers that might have been the empty shells of krill-like crustaceans. I leaned out from the main hatch and watched this sad procession. A man could sail a thousand miles, or ten thousand miles, and every single foot of the surface would yield up some residue of decay and renewal. Mostly it goes un-noticed.

The mist thickened again, bringing on a smattering of light rain. A black guillemot flew past and later, inevitably, a little auk. By midday we had covered just fourteen miles in twenty-four hours. A thin streak of blue sky appeared on the eastern horizon, somehow defying the enveloping fog, but never came any closer. I dropped the sail again, fed up with playing around to no benefit, and slept for an hour.

Nothing seemed to be happening, but the day was preparing itself for perhaps the most explosive moments of the whole voyage. The prelude to these moments was the arrival, mid-afternoon, of a slightly firmer current of air from the west. Refreshed by my nap, and ever the optimist, I raised seven panels of the sail. We pushed gently forwards through the mist. I heard a couple of hoarse, half-strangled barks and wondered whether there may be walruses about.

The breeze firmed up and so for the first time that day I was able to hook up the self-steering gear and release myself from helming with the steering lines. We were heading to the east-north-east, traversing therefore the southern coast of Kongsøya. Here I had to be careful, for a mass of rocks and small islands extends out the best part of ten miles from the wide southern bay of Kongsøya, the Breibukta. As far as I could make out from the chart, the most southerly hazard was a small rock called Nubbane, a couple of miles south of the last strip of island, Tirpizøya. To be sure of a good clearance from this rock I gybed and ran due east for a while, in a breeze which was now freshening and which soon had us down to four panels of sail. The fog was clearing too, revealing a sky heavy with cloud. The black cliffs of Kongsøya, indented with a series of ice gullies and wider glaciers, now dominated the northern horizon.

For more than a week I had been advancing with care and circumspection, and the appearance, to our south, of the first lump of drift ice of the voyage, now justified that caution. It was a moderate-sized floe, sculpted by time and intermittent melting into a jagged, crown-like form. There was something regal too in its unhurried progress south. I watched it and knew that our voyage had now changed. We had transgressed the limits of the sea ice, and so were entering the final phase of our outward journey.

Mignmij II Sails with Humpbacks

24

The encounter began innocuously enough. We had gybed back onto port tack to head north-east again, towards the eastern end of Kongsøya, in a breeze that was once more fading slowly. The evening was well advanced, but at this latitude in mid-summer, that meant nothing more than a slight reduction in the intensity of the light. The sun was still there, well masked by a covering of cloud, but it had declined to a shallow, less effective angle. Although midnight was only an hour or so away, we were still in broad but dull daylight.

My eye was drawn to some commotion ahead, signalled first by a gathering flock of agitated birds, and followed within a few seconds by several whale spouts. These were bushy, rectangular parcels of vapour, the typical spout of the humpback whale, and sure enough an unmistakable white fluke was raised skywards then disappeared. Another soon followed, and another. We were heading straight into a pod of leviathans.

At that moment, nothing seemed more appropriate. I recalled immediately my first visit to Jan Mayen, the first truly Arctic scene I had experienced, with its mix of mountain and ice and pulsing sea life, and my thought that all that was needed to complete the tableau was the raised fluke of a humpback whale. Here now was a remarkably similar scene. The line of cliffs to our north did not quite match the mountains of Jan Mayen in either grandeur or beauty, but they made up for that deficiency by the power of their bleakness and by their far more impressive air of remoteness. Here, we were almost five hundred miles closer to the North Pole. These islands spend most of the year locked into the pack-ice. Few humans ever come here. It was the perfect backdrop for a group of gambolling humpbacks.

The whales were milling about off our port bow, but some aspect of their general movement gave me the impression that they were heading the opposite way. On an impulse I disconnected the self-steering, put the helm down and brought us round onto the wind, so that we were now sailing along with the whales, perhaps a hundred yards ahead of them. I ducked down to grab a camera and a camcorder, sorted out the steering lines, and, standing in the hatchway, settled into our new course. I took a few photographs of the whales surfacing astern and waited to see what would happen.

I had assumed that the whales would quickly pass us, and that if I were lucky they might come close enough to enable me to get some decent images. I had no expectation that they would take any particular interest in *Mingming II*, still less that they would come in to examine her, and even less that they would absorb her into the pod and cruise companionably alongside, shoulder to shoulder.

After a few minutes spent with some distance between us and the whales, they started to move closer. By now I had dispensed with the camera and started filming with a camcorder, holding it in my right hand, while manipulating the steering lines with my left hand. Two whales, almost side by side, changed direction and angled in directly towards *Mingming II's* starboard quarter. At first I thought it was just a chance alteration of course, but it soon became clear that they were heading straight for us, and deliberately so. In they came, surfacing and breathing, almost in unison, every half minute or so, until they were right there, right under my nose, just a few feet off.

There are few things on this planet as thrilling as the proximity of a huge baleen whale. To sail along in the company of a pair of monsters getting on with their lives at the ends of the earth defies adequate description. All experience is stripped of relevance and meaning; the world and one's place in it is redefined at every level. Thought is reduced to tingling primeval sensation; there is nothing but the moment and its awful deliciousness.

Yes, it was truly terrifying to have two whales, each forty to fifty feet long, rolling their absurdly angled backs within a whisker of *Mingming II's* hull. I could not see their pectoral fins, but the port fin of the closest must have been almost beneath us. After each breath, the whales maintained themselves just a few feet below the surface. The air above was wild with screaming birds tracking their course, but I could follow their movement anyway, by the great circles of light-green aerated water produced by some minor activity of their blowholes. When they surfaced, I realised what an insipid descriptor the word blowhole is. These were massive apertures, the diameter of dustbins, ringed around with a huge donut of muscle. The thunderous discharge of steamy air, the spout itself, was the best part of two feet across. The escaping gas was just a blur, a rushing mass powered by a high-pressure hose of industrial proportions. With the wind angling in from ahead of us, I was spared the stink of this breath, although I would have welcomed it; it would have added another dimension to the overpowering impression of the moment. Just once, in the fraction of a second as the head of the nearest rolled forward, I caught a glimpse of the fist-sized tubercles, the hair follicles that sprout along the upper jaw.

The two whales off the quarter were joined by a third, a little further off and squarer on the beam, and so we were now four creatures of the sea, conjoined in a provisional harmony in the Arctic dusk. To the north, the cliffs and glaciers of Kongsøya overlaid the scene with an appropriate wildness. I was by now fully immersed in the power and strangeness of the moment; I had passed beyond care and thought into nothing but the unconditioned feeling of pure aliveness, a total absorption into the size and closeness and outrageous strength of these animals ranging alongside. For a moment I forgot the voyage, the mundane and temporal journeying across the sea. I forgot where I was and why I was there. The whole universe was now no more than these great mountains of living flesh: black, terrifying, noble, Jurassic; their scale and life-force overwhelming, humbling, totally mind-numbing. Yes, for a moment or two I felt a kind of ecstasy in the close company of those insanely beautiful monsters.

A man's body is an insistent partner and I was quickly brought back to earth by the increasing pain in my hands. The fingers of my right hand, in particular, now felt welded by cold to the camcorder. My shoulder, too, ached from the strain of holding the camera aloft. I had lost any sense of how long I had been standing out in the freezing Arctic air with little protection against it.

I pushed aside all thoughts of physical discomfort and concentrated once more on trying to etch into my mind the finer details of the whales still hugging close alongside. It was the anarchy in the shaping of their dorsal fins that fascinated me: the humpback fins had nothing of the beauty and

precision of form that characterise the dorsal fins of all the
other baleen whales. Each of the three whales had a dorsal fin
of a distinctly different profile. None of the fins resembled the
usual finely-curved crescent of the baleen whales. None was a
clean-lined falcate sickle sprouting straight from the smooth
plains of the whaleback. Each fin was arrived at by stages,
and each was somehow crudely misshapen and asymmetrical.
The whaleback itself was first enlarged by a long escarpment,
a smooth bump several metres long. Crowning this was a
second shorter and narrower excrescence that gave the back
a terraced look. The fin itself sprouted from this second
hummock. It started in an appropriate manner: a smooth blade
rising slowly. It was then that the anarchy and evolutionary
confusion began. In one of the whales the smooth line of
the blade became a series of angular steps, a kind of crudely
built staircase, as the fin rose to its apex. The top was squared
off: a long oblong box that fell away almost vertically. The
after edge of the fin, where one might have expected some
hydrodynamic scalloping, was no more than a ragged cliff
descending to the ridge that supported it. Another of the fins
was a little more inclined towards the crescent, but here again
it had all gone wrong: the fine point of the sickle had become
an outsized rounded globule. I wondered whether something
evolutionary and directed was going on here, whether several
configurations of the fin were competing for ascendancy, or
whether the cause of these disparities was something more
prosaic: damage caused by fighting or close scraping, for
example.

Slowly the whales pulled ahead and away from us; in the
light breeze our pace was too restrictive for them. I envied
them the clean simplicity of their life and their playground,
and was grateful for the gentleness of their examination of
Mingming II. In these waters they must rarely encounter
boats of any kind. Their curiosity had been piqued, they had

taken a long, peaceable look at us, and carried on unconcerned. They were heading west towards Svenskøya. After a final look at the whalebacks still rising in a regular rhythm, I went about and resumed our course to the north-east.

In those few minutes our voyage had been transformed; the whales had breathed a new life into the enterprise. For the first time I could start to feel the sense and shape of this particular adventure. It was too early to say whether this encounter might represent the defining motif of the whole journey, but I knew that whatever else happened, I now had something way beyond the normal and the expected to grasp on to; that I would go home a happy man.

Western End of Kongsøya from South East c. 25 miles.

25

The breeze faltered and swung round to the north-east, forcing us eastwards. I was still reeling from our communion with the whales and so cared little that we were being headed off course. Whether we meandered this way or that was of little import. All that mattered was that we were now here, absorbed into the life of this final wilderness. The rock and ice of Kongsøya, the last remnants of the terrestrial, still stretched across the northern horizon. Huge flocks of mewing kittiwakes infused the air with sound and movement. From time to time a whale spout fired off to our south. It was a timeless scene, and cold though I was, I could not quit the hatch and abandon myself to warmth and sleep. I had no choice but to maintain my vigil. The thought of missing anything of this moment was unbearable. Fourteen hundred miles of sailing had brought us to this place, to this moment. More than that, a lifetime of cause and effect, a whole concatenation of inexorable movement, a rich choreography that could only be understood in retrospect, had lead step by tiny step to these few hours at the ends of the earth. At the age of ten I had first seen the beckoning horizon from the deck of a small yacht. Almost sixty years of seemingly random experience, accumulated since that first moment of yearning, were now concentrated into this single instant. I felt a profound peace, because out of the senselessness of it all it was at least possible to discern a kind of coherent thread. Perhaps this was no more than an *a posteriori* illusion, a mental reordering that suited my own needs, but this in no way diminished the feeling that our presence there was the endpoint of a decades-long logical sequence. This explained, perhaps, the ease and rightness of the moment. Causality dictated that I could be at no other place than here. I was no more and no less than the person I had to be, doing what I had to do.

Eastern End of Kongsøya from South East c. 20 miles

26

Throughout the night we beat our way slowly towards the eastern extremity of Kongsøya, sometimes on port tack, sometimes on starboard, in a breeze that still could not settle. The sky was clearing slowly, allowing periods of brilliant and obliquely-angled sunshine. This light brought a blinding sparkle to the drifts of snow and ice that patterned the island. The blue of the sky turned the sea a deep indigo. With the cloud almost gone, along with its accompanying mist and heavy moisture, the air was now razor-sharp and vibrant.

A churning mass of bodies, throwing themselves along the surface of the sea, crossed our bow. At first I could not work out what they were; they seemed to be long-necked but headless, sea-beasts formed of nothing but a huge proboscis. Another group came in from a different angle, giving a better view. They were harp seals, close-packed and energetic, hurling themselves onto their right shoulders with each forward leap. A little later we passed by a whole line of them sleeping on their backs just beneath the surface, with just their muzzles poking through to the vital air above. They were lined up side by side with all the precision of a military dormitory.

A new belt of cloud passed over from the north, bringing with it a brief shower of heavy sleet. The wintriness of the moment was accentuated by the appearance of another ice floe working its way south further inshore. The sleet soon moved away, leaving Kongsøya laid out in total clarity from east to west. Here there was none of the grandiose impressiveness of Bjørnøya or Hopen; Kongsøya was more given to a subdued and subtle variety in its topography. It had its cliffs, and its glaciers, and a long spit stretching low to the south east. To the north-west it had sprouted a small conical mountain, sliced off at the top, this same feature echoed with less height and symmetry at the eastern end. It seemed likely that Kongsøya was a much older protrusion, and therefore more scarred and eroded by ice and time. This battered, worn-out look gave it more friendly, approachable aspect than its southern counterparts. It was somehow more messy, and modest, and therefore less threatening.

We made our way in to within a few miles of the island, and with the sun shining once more I was able to take a series of well-lit photographs. To the north-east I could start to make out the low-lying rock that constitutes the final island of the group, Abeløya. It was now less than five miles away, and was clearly little more than a flat reef. With the breeze now on the port quarter we bore away towards it.

We were by now within just a few miles of 79°North, and I still had no idea what I would do when we reached that meridian. My mind was still completely open to the two options of either continuing on north or turning round. Even a third lump of drift ice, gorgeously sculpted and translucent, that passed close by on our starboard side, failed to move me one way or the other. It was now a month since I had seen an ice map, and if the two previous years were a guide, the edge of the pack ice should by then have been well to our north. Somehow I did not feel that this was the case. We had so far encountered only three floes, but something in the air, some sixth sense perhaps, made me doubt that this year the north-east side of Svalbard had cleared itself of ice.

This impression was reinforced as Abeløya, such as it was, came clearly into view. It was nothing more than a ledge of rock just a metre or two high, its low perimeter fringed with ice. A sizeable iceberg dominated the line of black rock that now stretched across the north-east horizon. It was impossible to tell whether it was grounded on the northern shoreline, or whether it was stuck in one of the shallow bays that indent the island's eastern end. There it was, though, a sparkling lump of ice, the size of a house.

My failure to make a good record of the group of walruses I had seen further south still rankled, and I harboured a hope that Abeløya might provide the opportunity to make amends. As we neared the island I realised that this was unlikely. It was low-lying, but its edge was nonetheless a line of sheer and uninviting rock; there was no sloping beach that might induce walruses to haul out and congregate. It was a cruelly exposed spot too, with no prospect of any shelter. This was quickly becoming obvious as we moved into the lee of the island, just a mile or so offshore. The wind had veered a little to the north-west and was ratcheting itself up. What had been a pleasant breeze was turning to an uncompromising icy blast, laced with meaty squalls. This was cold, heavy air, viciously solid.

We were racing to the north-east, now under three panels, and our midday position put us less than three and a half miles from 79°North. Abeløya's fringe of rock and ice now stretched horizon to horizon on our port beam. There were no walruses, only kittiwakes in their hundreds, half of them airborne, the other half littering the sea in tight-packed flocks. The wind thundered in with a pure and icy bleakness, whipping up the surface into fast-moving patches of water so dark they were almost black.

Just forty-five minutes after midday on Wednesday the thirtieth of July, after twenty-six days at sea, we reached 79°North and I decided to turn round. This decision, when it came, was made rapidly, and was driven by a sudden convergence of three factors. Looking aloft, I saw that the rig had suffered its first failure of the voyage. The after end of the second batten down had chewed its way through its heavily hand-sewn restraining pocket, and was now poking out by several inches. The battens keep the sail panels nicely stretched, and so the sail was now slack and bunched up in that area. The sooner I could repair the pocket and get the batten working properly again, the better. The wind was still strengthening, though; there was no prospect of making a repair until I had calmer conditions. I reduced sail to just two panels, to take the affected batten out of service and reduce the chances of the damage becoming worse. Increasingly vicious squalls of frigid air were thumping in every half minute or so, and I would soon have had to reef anyway. With the rig no longer in full working order, and with the weather deteriorating, I was already feeling hesitant about carrying on north. A scan of the northern horizon made up my mind. There was ice up there; not just small floes, but sizeable icebergs. We had come as far as was reasonable, and within a minute or two I had put *Mingming II* about and settled her in to her new course to the south-west.

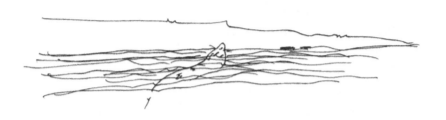

27

It was, in a way, a release. For nearly a month the over-riding question had been: how far north will we be able to sail? I had constructed a thousand imaginary scenarios, taking us anywhere from the Victoria Sea to an anti-clockwise circumnavigation of Svalbard. Now, circumstance had conspired to define the outer limit of our voyage. I had no regret at turning south at 79°North. For *Mingming II* to have equalled *Mingming's* highest latitude of 80°North, on her maiden voyage, would perhaps have been impertinent. In any case, I had a deep sense that to have carried on north would have been over-stretching what was reasonable or indeed prudent. This sense proved correct, for the ice that year clung on stubbornly to the north-east corner of Svalbard. The ice map for the day I turned south showed that we were less than sixty miles from the edge of the pack-ice. Kvitøya, Victoria Island, all of Franz Josef Land and the Victoria Sea were still ice-bound, and would remain so for the whole summer. To have pushed on north would have brought danger without any hope of reward.

I turned south, then, with a clear conscience and a light heart. Now we were free to play. Nowhere was off limits between Kong Karls Land and Whitehills, fifteen hundred miles to our south. We were by now at home in the High Arctic. *Mingming II*, fast in light airs and easily managed, was proving the ideal yacht for the conditions. With the limits of the ice now defined I could relax a little and enjoy exploring these outlandish islands. We had time aplenty at our disposal, and so could wander home at leisure, poking our nose into whichever corners the wind allowed us to approach.

The outward, northern leg of an Arctic voyage is always burdened by the thought that every mile sailed will have to be re-done in the other direction; for every mile sailed north at least two are added to the total voyage. Now that we had turned south, the doubling factor had gone. Each mile home was now a pure mile. The miles seemed lighter, less encumbered by the weight of having to make a return. They *were* the return.

We had reached the most northerly latitude of the voyage and, in all likelihood, the coldest conditions. I therefore allowed myself the luxury of putting on my warmest sweater. Up until that point I had been holding it back, to force my body to acclimatise to the cold, and to have something extra-warm in reserve should we meet even lower temperatures. It was my Faroese fisherman's sweater, found a few years earlier in a little shop in Brighton, and saved for just this day. It was hand-knitted in thick soft wool, exquisitely patterned and supernaturally warm. At 79°North I had been wearing two pairs of socks, underpants, long johns, track suit bottoms, a long-sleeved woollen vest, a cotton polo shirt, a light fleece and a heavy fleece. I now interposed the Faroese sweater between the two fleeces.

Disgracefully warm, I thought more about my two sister ships, *Mingming* and *Mingming II*. They were of course half-sisters rather than full sisters: two daughters by different mothers. *Mingming* was perhaps the prettier of the two: a petite, light-framed and graceful blonde, but a tough blonde nonetheless who had shown her worth over and over. *Mingming II* was the big, no-nonsense brunette; athletic, fast, self-assertive and radical. Like her little sister, she too was scared of nothing. Together they had taken most of Svalbard in an almost symmetrical pincer movement, and I was proud of them.

We were now on an almost reciprocal course, heading south-west past Kongsøya and Svenskøya towards Kapp Melchers, the north-east shoulder of Edgeøya. For weeks I had been puzzled by a feature of my chart: much of this area of Edgeøya's coast was delineated by a long dotted line. I was not sure what this meant. It was undoubtedly something to do with ice, as a large portion of the island is covered by a massive ice-cap, the Edgejøkulen, and this line marked the seaward edge of the ice-cap. On our northerly trajectory I had kept well clear of this area. Now was the time to examine it more closely.

For twelve hours we reached quickly south-west in a searingly cold half gale. We were down to just a single panel of sail and I was glad we had turned south: I would not have liked to have encountered ice in these conditions. There were whales about, firing off spouts of quickly-dispersed moisture, and tracked by huge flocks of kittiwakes screaming their *kaka-weeek, kaka-weeek* lament. In the rough seas nothing could be seen of the whales themselves.

Heavy weather rarely lasts long in the High Arctic summer, and by midnight the wind was easing. By four-thirty the next morning we were becalmed, and I was able to make a temporary repair to the errant batten. It was not possible while under way to force it back into its proper position and re-sew its pocket. It was important, though, to restrain the batten from working its way further out of the sail. I scoured a hole in the batten's carbon fibre tubing with the sharp point of my multi-tool, fed a short length of 6mm line through the hole, and sewed the line to the webbing tabling of the sail leech. This would hold the batten firmly in position.

We lay under a grey sky, with Kongsøya twenty miles or so to the north-west. I sketched the contours of the island in the ship's log. A minke whale sidled past, followed by an Iceland gull, pure white, fine-winged, superbly graceful. The bustle of the previous twenty-four hours had evaporated, leaving us once more to a world in suspension. We rolled and creaked to a gentle swell. A tiny seal head broached the surface and was quickly gone. Not yet ready for sleep I kept up my vigil.

Seal

28

The Arctic winds resumed their fitful gentleness. Soft breezes caressed us from here and there, and then disappeared. The sun maintained its tight parabola behind a veil of shredded cloud. The islands of Kong Karls Land lay low on the northern horizon, receding imperceptibly. Our progress to the south-west was interspersed with long periods of immobility on a grey and placid sea.

We were tracked by a party of fifteen or so harp seals. They had perhaps never seen a yacht, and seemed unable to contain their inquisitiveness. During the calms they played a cat-and-mouse game with us, torn between curiosity and caution. This game was played for hours and invariably followed the same format. The first phase was the approach. For this the seals separated out and came in towards us underwater. Well spread out, they poked their heads out for a second or two, had a short look at us, and then sank back below the surface. The bolder ones came within a few yards of *Mingming II*. This observation phase usually lasted five or ten minutes. Sometimes they sidled along the surface for a second or two before disappearing with a quick flick of their tail. Occasionally a seal forced itself almost upright out of the water, the better to see, somehow defying gravity as it hung there almost fully exposed. This manoeuvre was usually made at a safe distance, and just once or twice three or four seals managed it simultaneously.

It was the final retreat phase that fascinated me. It was impossible to tell what triggered this, but after a few minutes of observing us with consummate stealth, the signal was given for a group withdrawal. The scattered seals rejoined each other, forming a tight-knit group, and sped off together along the surface with a great commotion and much splashing. This noisy retreat seemed to be saying: *Right, we're off now! Good-bye! Look at us, we're going now! See that? We're off! Bye!* Five minutes later a head popped up alongside and the cycle recommenced. This round of approach and retreat carried on for as long as we were becalmed.

The seals were quick and elusive, but after hours of careful observation I was able develop a clear picture of their physical characteristics. In form they were, as I have said, long-necked and small-headed. The line of the neck ran straight into the outline of the skull, and so from certain angles, in particular from the rear, they seemed headless. Their eyes were deep-set and large, and oversaw a black, distinctly dog-like and heavily-whiskered muzzle. Lower down, the neck flared out into a fat body that itself finally narrowed to the double tail flipper, the last echo of ancient hind legs. In evolutionary terms, these harp seals seemed on their way to achieving the shape and sleekness of sea-lions. Their coloration, though, has gone in a completely different direction. Their fur is an exquisite shade of dark silver, overlaid with a delicate champagne sheen, and patterned, on the back and neck, with randomly sized and oddly shaped black spots.

I made sketches of the seals, and of the mechanics of their way of racing along the surface. Once up to speed they launched themselves into the air, making regular looping leaps, dolphin-like. Each leap ended in disarray, as the seals threw themselves clumsily onto their right shoulders when landing, creating great flurries of spray and, on a quiet day, a constant sound of churning water.

A hint of a breeze started up from the north-north-west, and so we pulled away slowly under seven panels of the sail. The cliffs of Svenskøya were still there, low on the north-east horizon, but now my eyes were searching ahead. We were crossing the southern end of the Olgastretet, heading straight for the north-east corner of Edgeøya, now not much more than thirty miles away. To the north of Edgeøya was the smaller island of Barentsøya, it too ice-capped and rising to a height of nearly two thousand feet. It would not be long before the first hints of these islands hove into view.

Sure enough, at just after three in the afternoon of the first of August, our twenty-ninth day at sea, the highest peak of Barentsøya, the Schweinfurthberget, poked above the north-west horizon. Within a few minutes one of Edgeøya's topmost points, the Middendorfberget, was bearing due west, followed swiftly by the grey whalebacks of the Edgejøkulen, Edgeøya's mighty ice-cap. The sky was clearing from the north-west, revealing new peaks and ice-slopes across the whole of the western horizon.

Before long the upper contours of Barentsøya and Edgeøya were laid out end to end. I knew that between the two, not far to our north-west, lay the Freemansundet, the narrow strait that separates the two islands. It was here that Bill Tilman had re-ballasted his pilot cutter *Baroque* in 1974, after being forced to jettison her ballast when he ran onto a reef at the strait's eastern end. Three tons of pig-iron had been ferried ashore, to be replaced later with a similar volume, if not weight, of large stones hauled off the Freemansundet beach. It was heart-warming to be mooching around so close to this scene of heroic seamanship.

The sky, for the moment, was ridding itself of cloud, and so the evening sun had full play on the rolling prairie of ice that covers most of Edgeøya. Gentle slopes folded themselves higher and higher towards the centre of the island, creating a thousand square miles of sparkling ice-cap. As we closed the shore-line I started to divine what was meant by the dotted line on my chart: the fields of ice met the sea with a sheer cliff-face. We were sailing in towards the most northerly section of ice-cliff, which runs on an east-west axis for ten miles or so, and here the ice fell vertically into the sea. It was hard to calculate the exact height of theses cliffs; it was somewhere between seventy and a hundred feet. In the low-angled sun the face of the cliffs glowed a blinding white. Later I would learn that this northern stretch also has a strong green component in its colouring.

Ten miles off, the breeze deserted us. There was nothing to do but lower and lash the mainsail, and sleep for a while. I had already decided that I would sail in as close as I dared to the edge of the glacier. If that meant waiting for the right wind, then so be it. I turned in and slept for three hours.

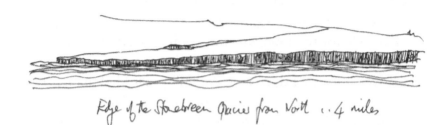

Edge of the Storebreen Glacier from North c. 4 miles

29

In general I prefer to keep a healthy offing, especially when sailing in remote areas. Risks tend to rise in direct proportion to one's proximity to land. This is especially so for the engineless sailor. There are some sights, though, that are so magnetic, and so demanding of close-up examination, that they induce the need to take a higher level of risk.

I had never before seen a glacier of these proportions, and never before seen miles of ice-cliffs. To have kept my usual distance would have been unthinkable. I needed to sail in close, to observe, to photograph and film, to try to get a real sense of the scale and power of this mile-thick blanket of frozen water. I needed to know what it felt like to have trillions of tons of ice towering overhead. I wanted to observe and record every detail of the cliff's configuration, to understand its form and its colour. I wanted to see what went on its base, at the interface between the ice and the ocean. Clearly, I could not touch the glacier, but maybe I could smell it and listen to its respirations, and perhaps feel its coldness.

To make the best of a close approach to a dangerous coastline, two things are needed: an appropriate wind and good light; the former to minimise navigational problems, the latter to maximise the photographic possibilities. Although in one sense the safest wind is an offshore wind, as one can turn tail and run off easily in any direction, it is in fact less than ideal. The major difficulty is that the closer one approaches, the less the wind, especially when the coastline is high and steep. An offshore wind can be very fickle too, both in strength and direction. When close in to high cliffs, sailing can become almost impossible, with long calm patches interspersed with thudding squalls from almost any direction. If the land is ice-bound, the general anarchy of the wind can be magnified; ice seems too to encourage a particular viciousness in the gusts.

A more reliable wind is usually one blowing parallel with the line of the coast. Such a wind is generally firmer close in, and more consistent. One can reach in easily, and reach away just as quickly. If the wind is in the general direction of travel, one can run before the wind, parallel with the coast, but always with the ability to head quickly offshore if necessary.

As a general rule I never approach a remote coastline, for purely observational purposes, with an onshore wind.

It is rare to have a combination of a well-placed sailing breeze and good light for photography. There is always the option, of course, of heaving-to and waiting for the right conditions. I have on many occasions convinced myself that I am going to do just that: simply wait it out. In practice I find my patience runs out within twenty-four hours. One could be waiting for a week to no avail. Although speed is of little interest, and there is nothing wrong with a protracted calm, there is still that underlying urge to keep moving, to be getting on. All one can do is make the best of the immediate conditions; one can always return another time.

We lay a few miles off the north-east corner of the Stonebreen, the Stone Glacier, and waited to see what the new day would bring. The sky closed in again, carrying with it mist, and then rain. Through the heavily moisture-laden air the ice-cap and the cliffs took on a grey-green, grainy aspect. There was no hint of glint or sparkle. It was a dull, sodden scene, verging on the hopeless for photography. I was not dismayed, having long since rid myself of unreasonable expectation. In any case, the weather hereabouts was in constant flux.

When the breeze came in, gently at first, it came from the north, almost perfect for running south along the main stretch of the ice-cliffs. With five panels set we ghosted in towards the coast. Four miles off, I went about again. The wind was as yet unconvincing, and I dared not risk losing directional control any closer to the ice. As yet I had no sense of the set of the local currents, and we were still too far off for me to assess the ice floes that must inevitably be carving from the glacier's edge. Better to be patient than to rush on into an awkward trap.

We hung around for a while, just inside the mouth of the Blåbukta, the north-easternmost bay of Edgeøya, an indent defined by Kapp Heuglin at its northern extremity, and Kapp Melchers, a headland composed of nothing but ice, at its southern end. By eleven in the morning the wind had firmed a little, and so I resumed the run in towards Kapp Melchers. The intention was to cut obliquely past the cape as close as I dared. The light was still very poor, but by now we had a steady breeze on the starboard quarter. It might be our only chance to sail in close in reasonable safety.

The north-facing ice-cliffs fell vertically into the sea, but there was nothing smooth or regular about the cliff-face.

The ice was fissured with a crazed pattern of vertical cracks, some shallow, some quite deep. Secondary splits ran at more horizontal angles between the principal fissures. At one point, more or less at Kapp Melchers itself, a dark and deep cave had somehow been created, reaching almost to the top of the cliff. The ice was everywhere rough and knobbly, riven by a maze of cracks and deformations. The detail was anarchic, but this anarchy was repeated along a five mile stretch, and so the overall effect was of something harmonious and inevitable. The ice glowed from within with the green of tarnished copper. In places it had turned reddish-brown, perhaps where the ice had swept up something geological in its path. In the poor light the surface of the glacier, stretching away inland, looked grey-brown and mucky. It was hard to see whether this was the colour of the ice itself, or whether the ice was covered with a layer of detritus; stones or grit or perhaps volcanic ash. Further south the surface was more distinctly patched, suggesting that the ice was indeed partially littered with rock of some sort. There was no question that in bright sunlight the whole scene would transform to blinding brilliance, but for the moment it was a strangely muted glacier, subdued and gloomy.

We sailed in closer. I broke out the lead line and made the occasional heave. I had no idea whether there may be a tongue of ice projecting out from the glacier beneath the surface. It seemed likely. The water was turning to an icy green, the colour of melt-water, and so it seemed wise to check the depth from time to time. I found no bottom. For a few minutes a thinning overhead improved the light, but the heavier cloud soon returned, and with it rain. I tacked seawards again, to hold position and see if conditions would improve.

Towards five in the afternoon, after twenty hours of jilling back and forth, with the light still poor but lifted by a patch or two of blue sky astern, we made our definitive run in to the glacier. I approached slowly, still heaving the lead from time to time. Now I no longer needed binoculars to see the detailing of the ice, with all its intricate sculpting, or to appreciate its ghostly green glow. More importantly, I could now see what was happening close in to the base of the cliffs. A stream of ice floes and bergy bits was being carried steadily north. This was the crucial navigational information I needed, and it put me on very high alert. The closer I went in, the greater the danger of losing the wind and being subsumed into this north-going parade of ice. This was a prospect best avoided.

I kept on in, nonetheless, as the breeze was holding, and I still wanted to cut across the apex of Kapp Melchers. The cape itself was indented with a couple of small bays, and the southern side of the first bay marked a distinct change in the nature of the ice-cliffs. For a start they rose higher than the northern stretch, reaching to perhaps a hundred feet. The face of the ice was now no longer sheer, but had a crumbled, crumpled look. This rugged, collapsed aspect continued for the thirty miles to the southern end of the glacier. Here the ice was cleaner and brighter, and was suffused with blue rather than green. My impression was that it was here, along the main east-facing section of the ice-cliffs, that the interaction between ice and sea was more active. Here the ice was breaking and falling, and therefore regularly revealing fresh, new-minted surfaces. The north-facing segment had a more static, immutable look to it, and so here the ice was old and stained.

We rounded Kapp Melchers a mile or so offshore, and for a while had the whole glacier lain out before us: five miles of ice-cliffs running away due west, and thirty more miles of unbroken ice trailing off into the murk to our south. The inland whalebacks of the glacier were lost in the persistent low cloud.

I now had a clear view down the line of the cliff-face, and so could make a better assessment of the inshore current and the ice it was carrying. The stream of ice seemed confined to within about half a mile of the shore-line. I had a brief moment of concern when I thought I saw some outlying rocks. Nothing was marked on the chart. The rocks were seals, hitching a ride on the ice floes.

There was one other navigational consideration. A group of rocks and small islands, the Ryke Yseøyane, lies about ten miles offshore halfway between Kapp Melchers and the glacier's southern end. I had to make a decision whether to pass inside, or to give the islands a clear berth to seawards. My natural preference was of course to keep well offshore. For all the softness of the day this was a wild and unforgiving part of the world. I was on my own, willingly and uncompromisingly; if something went wrong there would be no easy escape. For once my well-honed survival instinct was over-ruled. I wanted to sail down the whole length of the glacier as close in as I dared. We settled in about a mile and a half offshore and started the long run south.

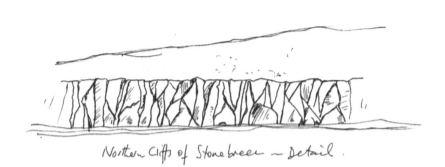

Northern Cliffs of Stonebreen — Detail.

30

Ice was imitating land; ice had become land. From north to south there was nothing but ice become cliffs, and to the west the ice fields rolled away and up into the clouds. It was ice on a colossal scale; a whole tectonic plate of ice; ice parading as landscape.

It was bewildering. Here was a thousand square miles of ice, and, for all I knew, a thousand *cubic* miles of ice, formed, I assumed, from nothing but compacted snow. There is something easily assimilable about sea-ice: the surface of the sea freezes and forms an icy crust. That is not too difficult to conceive of. But these cliffs, these mountains of ice; this was a different matter. It was beyond conception: the time required, the accrual of infinitesimally small layers of snow, the melting and re-freezing, the compacting, the transformation of soft crystals into rock-hard ice; a whole topography constructed molecule by molecule over aeons too long to contemplate. I tried to imagine how many blizzards, over how many years, it had taken to assemble this ice-cap; how many thousands, or hundreds of thousands, of winter storms and brief summer warmings had been required to create such a monolith. How had it all begun? Somewhere under this mass was the residue of a previous, proper landscape. Was it a single landmass or an Arctic archipelago? Was it once temperate here? Did flowers bloom? Did ruminants graze? Was it forested? How many overarching cycles of freezing and warming, of death and rebirth, had tempered the land and the ocean? Was this already incomprehensible ice-cap simply one in an endless series?

I thought about the rock still buried somewhere beneath the ice. A rough calculation put the weight of a thousand cubic miles of ice at nearly four billion tons. The compressive force of this weight must surely be pushing the land down. I remembered reading that during our own Ice Age the weight of ice had titled the British mainland on a north-south axis, and that the north of Britain, now released from its burden, is slowly rising back to equilibrium. This brought me back to my long-held thought that the only constant is the ocean. Land is ever-shifting and ephemeral; so too is ice.

Despite its scale and seeming solidity, I knew that the glacier was moving. I could hear it. The ice was murmuring and groaning, and every few minutes let out a rumbling roar, sometimes a distant roll of thunder, sometimes a sharp-edged artillery salvo. A battle was being played out up on the slopes as the ice-sheet buckled and turned and slid its way down to the sea, forcing its way over the rock beneath. No doubt the individual movements were infinitesimal: a thousandth of an inch here and there, but each microscopic shift set off a great graunching. Perhaps the ice acted as its own sounding board, magnifying the momentary vibrations caused by its incessant grinding. Having thus become vocal, the ice had taken on a kind of persona. It was unnerving, this icescape lain out from horizon to horizon, moaning and bellowing in its uneasy sleep.

I have seen the bare moraines of long-dead glaciers, and the sad tongues of expiring glaciers receding back up their slopes. The Stonebreen seemed in good health, but I feared that it too was sick at heart, that its restlessness was a symptom of an accelerated rate of melting, that its grumblings and growlings were the first sign of a drawn out agony.

Eastern Cliffs of Storebreen — Detail

31

For ten hours we ran south, tracing the line of the cliffs. Everywhere, on this eastern face, they had crumbled; huge chunks of ice littered the base of the cliff-face, sometimes piling up almost to its topmost point. The cloud was still thick and low, and the light opaque, and so the surface of the glacier retained its mucky look. As we crossed the line between the glacier and the outlying Ryke Yseøyane, the ice cliff turned a dirty brown. At this point the ice had clearly been working over rock and shale, sweeping it up and swallowing it into the glacier's structure. It made sense: there was probably a ridge here that extended out to the islands. This was confirmed on the chart by a patch of shallower water directly offshore.

The breeze was easing, but still we ran on. The mountain that marks the southern end of the glacier solidified through the haze. This shoulder of rock, perhaps seven or eight hundred feet high and two or three miles wide, had been enough to contain the pressure of the ice and force the glacier seawards. It had split the movement of the ice from the uplands; to its south was the smaller Kong Johans Breen, a mere four miles wide. Further south an imperious ridge of mountains stretched away.

Towards ten in the evening the wind swung round to the south-west and dropped to almost nothing. Reluctantly I headed offshore; if we were to be becalmed I wanted sea room. Nothing gave any indication that the light was going to improve. We had come as close in to the ice as was prudent, but my photographs and film were dull and grainy. This was a legitimate mood of the glacier, probably its predominant one, but I would have liked to have captured the ice in full sparkle.

With a faint breeze on the beam we drew away to the south-east. I had been on watch for nearly twenty-four hours and it was time to sleep. We were heading offshore in deserted waters and so, had I wanted, I could have slept long and deeply. My sub-conscious was by then too well honed to alertness to allow a total relaxation; the sailor's imperative to check and check again was too well ingrained. At midnight, after little more than an hour in my bunk, I woke and looked astern. *Oh!* It was scarcely credible. Much of the cloud had evaporated, leaving swathes of blue overhead. The midnight sun, low to the north-east, had the cliffs of Kong Johans Breen in its sights, turning them to a strip of blinding white. The higher slopes of the ice cap were patched with sunlight. There were rolls of mist playing along the declivities of the land, and the sky to the north was still marred by a thick layer of stratus, but the transformation was startling. This was the light I had been waiting for.

I went about and settled us back on a reciprocal course, heading straight for the ice-cliffs of Kong Johans Glacier. I hoped to get in close, to have them towering overhead in full brilliance, to catch every nuance of their form and colour, to capture the intricacy of the light and shade created by their pitted, fissured surface. We sailed in, and I filmed and photographed as we went. The breeze was blowing from the high mountains to the south, and as we closed the coast it faltered. Three miles off we were becalmed. The set of the current was to the north, angling in towards the ice-cliffs. I had no choice but to go about, and with seven panels set, start the slow job of once more working our way offshore. The priority was, at the very least, to counteract the current. The further we were carried inshore, under the lee of the cliffs, the less wind we would have and the less chance of escape.

It was the moment for *Mingming II's* mighty sail to show its mettle. In a placid sea, Mediterranean azure under the morning sun, the sail's upper panels harnessed the tiniest movements of air to give a hint of momentum. Almost imperceptibly, we eased away. Astern, the mighty whaleback of ice, a smooth undulation rising higher and higher inland, now spanned almost the whole of the western horizon. Only the coastal ramparts hid its southern extremity. Off to the north, stretches of the Stonebreen cliffs glistened in the early morning sun. The ice reflected and magnified the sunlight, and for a while it lost its wintriness. Sandwiched between a blue sky and a blue sea and sparkling benignly, the glacier somehow radiated warmth and friendliness. Perhaps it was as well the wind had failed; the temptation to sail in too close may have been irresistible. It was a siren beauty, this beauty of the ice, provisional and deadly, and better watched from a safe distance. I yearned for a closer embrace, yes, but good sense intervened. This was not the time for a gesture of the heart.

We pulled slowly away, and as we came out of the lee of the mountains the breeze strengthened. Our course was to the south, back towards Hopen. I wanted to explore its western side. Perhaps, too, we might once more encounter walruses.

The eastern side of Edgeøya, as far north as Kapp Melchers, was now laid out under the morning sun. Sated with the glacier, I turned my attention to the heights that stretched away south from Kong Johans Glacier. This range, Stone's Forland, typified the coastal mountains of eastern Svalbard. A low shoreline rose slowly for half a mile or so, then steepened into semi-sheer scree. Above this towered corrugated buttresses, long and flat-topped. For the first time I could see how the vertical corrugations were formed. The deeper, more sheltered gullies still held patches of ice. Each patch was a kind of miniature glacier, working its way down its individual couloir and eroding the rock as it went. There was clearly a feed-back system working here: the more deeply the ice penetrated into the face of the rock, the less it was exposed to the sun and to melting, and so the more effective it became. The shallower corrugations were bare; it was only the deeper ones that still held inverted triangles of ice. Only one or two of these triangles reached to the foot of the mountains; most were receding upwards. Further south, all that remained were narrow patches just under the lip of the plateau.

Inevitably, the line of the mountain had been pierced by the occasional full-blown glacier. The most northerly of these, just a mile or two south of Kong Johans Glacier, still held a wide river of ice, but the river no longer reached the sea; its melting tongue stopped short about half a mile from the water. The glaciers further south were no more than bare moraines.

Seals Keeping us Company; Svenskøya to North

32

The south-westerly took us away from Edgeøya and into the roll of thick mist that had appeared on the southern horizon. There was something almost comforting about being once more back into this shrouded world. It was not a heavy, persistent fog; from time to time it thinned, revealing the long line of mountains that dominated the southern end of Edgeøya. The wind faltered again and by mid-afternoon we were once more becalmed.

It was a happy calm. For a start we were almost equidistant from Edgeøya and Hopen, giving us plenty of sea room. Our drift was now to the south-east, out into the Barents Sea, and so in no way threatening. Hopen was not yet visible, but its presence was hinted at by a concentration of white cumulus rising above the band of sea mist ahead. The moisture-laden air was not dense enough to block the sun or the blue of the sky; it acted more as a softening filter. The play of the sun's rays created a whole vocabulary of prismatic effects, from full-blown rainbows to tiny shimmering patches of colour. It was soothing, this equilibrium between illuminated mist and restrained sunshine. The Edgeøya glacier was still talking to us, grumbling away from time to time.

Feeling thus at ease, and in no hurry, and by now thoroughly at home, I took to house-keeping. Using the boat-hook I retrieved the water-proof bags full of clothes from the depths of the port aft stowage, and selected a wardrobe of fresh things to wear. It was a rare total change, executed in one session. The used clothes were bagged and stowed forward. Refreshed and dapper, I moved on to other periodic tasks. I cleaned and refuelled the stove. I calculated my remaining water: thirty-eight litres. I exited the hatch and re-tensioned the self-steering lines. While out there I checked over the Windpilot, making sure that nothing was working loose.

Chores finished, I watched the world. Here was nothing but sea, mist and distant rock, but it was more than enough. To have the world thus simplified brought it into sharper focus. Marooned in an Arctic calm, I could better sense the essence of things. Here was the eternal play of the inanimate: earth, air and water. This was the history of the planet, with we crawling, animate things no more than a provisional side-show. It was a bleak and liberating thought: humankind central to nothing except its own hubris.

I watched, too, the Brünnich's guillemots. They were here in their thousands. Flocks streamed one way or the other in endless procession, hour after hour. In the soft sunlight their underbellies glowed with a brilliant, blinding white, the enhanced and almost supernatural white of soap powder advertisements. Even if they played rugby on muddy pitches, these guillemots would come off spotless. They were too unwaveringly earnest, though, for the frivolity of sport. For them there was no let-up from the imperatives of survival and reproduction.

I admired their single-mindedness. Their flight was direct and rapid, usually low over the water, occasionally a little higher. There was never the slightest hesitation or variation in their speed. If a flock passed close by I could hear the rush of air through feathers; sometimes I fancied I could hear the workings of the musculature that produced its blur of wing beats. These birds speeding along, hour after hour, back and forth, in total silence and harmony, getting on with what they had to do, without reflection, without complaint, epitomised a pure and unmediated will-to-live. Their movement and energy was incessant, their driving force unrelenting. I felt dull and sluggish by comparison; leaden.

It was the same old problem: too much thinking. I could watch these birds for days on end, and find in their behaviour a thousand metaphors for bigger, less important things. For their part, they rushed past and saw *Mingming II* and her alien skipper and couldn't give a damn. This is not to say they were devoid of all inquisitiveness. Once in a while it was possible to detect a slight deviation in course that brought a flock in closer. This movement towards was balanced by movement away; some flocks veered off, driven by a predominance of caution.

On just one occasion, a large squadron of birds headed straight for us, low on the starboard beam, and kept coming. At the last moment it peeled off left and right, in aeronautical symmetry, to form two groups, one passing astern, the other ahead. For a second or two the party at the bow stalled itself in mid-flight, as if to take a better look, before accelerating off, back to the business of food, reproduction and genetic immortality.

The size of the flocks ranged from a couple of birds to perhaps sixty or seventy. Years of observation had brought me no closer to determining how these flocks formed themselves. Nor could I work out what controlled their direction of flight. Clearly they operated between two poles: their nesting sites and their feeding grounds, but their flight-paths criss-crossed at random angles. I could only surmise that as the birds flew off from the cliffs where they nested, they formed random groups, with single birds joining one by one, perhaps for protection. The flocks had no specific leader. Perhaps they broke up in reverse manner: individual birds peeling off one by one to start their hunting. I saw one curious incident: a lone bird veered off from an outbound flock, and with a rapid u-turn appended itself to a flock going the other way.

For almost a day and a night, as we lay in a misty calm, I watched the guillemots racing back and forth. There was never a second's let-up; on and on they went, tirelessly. Every bird was identical, each one a perfectly formed Prince Charles, or Karl Marx, or Marilyn Monroe.

Just after midday on the fourth of August, after a day's run of just thirteen miles, a faint breeze started up from the south-south-east. With the full sail set we moved off again, ghosting to the west of south.

The wind was heading us away from Hopen and I began to think about an alternative plan. I spread out the chart of southern Svalbard and studied it closely. If we were to be pushed to the west I had to be careful: a string of rocks and small islands extended out a long way from the southern tip of Edgeøya. This was an area to keep well clear of. Further to the west lay the great fjord that separates Edgeøya from Spitsbergen itself, the Storfjorden. Perhaps we could stick our nose in there. A little to the south of west, a hundred miles or so away, was the southern tip of Spitsbergen, the Sorkapp. That too might be worth looking at. The Spitsbergen coast to the north-east of the Sorkapp looked well-glaciered and interesting. There were lots of possibilities. As ever I kept an open mind. In any case, for the moment we were scarcely moving. Content in my work I hung out of the after hatch and watched the endless procession of princely birds.

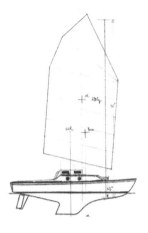

33

I had now spent more than a month at sea aboard *Mingming II*. To sail her and to live aboard her was so smooth and effortless that she has become an almost silent partner in this narrative. Save for the one failure of an aft batten pocket at 79°North, there had been almost nothing to upset the easy flow of our progress. The one minor irritation was the tendency of the main sheet and the sheet spans to twist. This is a common characteristic of rope in general, rather than something specific to *Mingming II*, and try as I might, I could not induce the sheet and spans to stay untwisted for any length of time. This twisting hindered the smooth run of the sheet through the blocks. If I wanted to let the mainsheet out, I sometimes had to grab an upper part of the sheet and overhaul it manually through the blocks to create some slack. I like things to look as they should, good and seamanlike, and found the sight of these twists, sometimes building to four or five on each side of a block, offensive to the eye. Whenever conditions allowed, I un-rove parts of the mainsheet and ran the twists out of the rope with my hands, but this did little good. I needed to lay the whole rope out lengthways, all eighty feet or so of it, and work at it for an hour to settle it down.

I like a boat to be dry, and had put in many hours of work to ensure that *Mingming II* was absolutely watertight. This had paid off: after a month at sea the bottom of the bilge had nothing more than a slight film of dampness. This dampness came not from leaks, but from condensation. The interior insulation had eliminated most, but not all, of the boat's potential condensation. The only place where droplets of moisture gathered was on the aluminium frames of the three hatches. This only caused annoyance at the central hatch, as from time to time a drip or two fell onto the leeward bunk. This was fresh water, in tiny amounts, which dried quickly and completely. Whenever condensation built up, when I was cooking or the hatches were closed, I ran a piece of kitchen wipe over the frame to soak up the moisture.

The aft stowage area under the cockpit and aft side-decks was also prone to condensation, as it would have taken too much time and trouble to insulate the inaccessible and awkwardly shaped deck-head here. I had insulated the hull itself, and that certainly helped, but the underside of the deck and cockpit generated moisture from time to time. It was here that I stored my clothes, and having fresh dry clothes available when needed is a boon to comfort. I had long since learned that even watertight bags can become damp inside, in high latitudes, again because of condensation. All individual items inside these bags were wrapped tightly in plastic bags before being packed. This kept them bone dry for months.

The one area of the hull and coach roof that I had not insulated was the observation pod. The sides of this were constructed in inch-thick laminated plywood, and the top in one inch solid timber with a thin plywood sheathing. The substantial framing was a mix of solid hardwoods and pine. I had suspected that there was enough thickness here not to require insulation. It was somehow comforting, and helped give *Mingming II's* cabin a proper yacht feel, to have an area of natural timber always visible, and so I had decided to leave it bare and see what happened. Timber is a poor conductor, and sure enough, the inside of the observation pod stayed moisture-free.

I had no problems keeping reasonably warm. The strategy of forcing my body to acclimatise to the colder ambient temperatures soon paid off. At no time during the voyage did I have to resort to what I might consider a full Arctic rig: thickly layered clothing topped with a heavy snow-boarding jacket and padded ski trousers. I had a couple of Russian-style faux-fur hats with me, and always wore one of them inside the cabin. Keeping the head warm is important. For working at the hatch, or going on deck, I invariably put on my lined waterproof baseball-type hat, with a fold-down flap that covers ears and neck. I had sewn a length of light line to this to make a chin-strap, and fashioned a leather toggle, and so there was little risk of it being blown off.

To be able to pass my time in just a few layers of loose clothing, with a couple of pairs of thick socks to keep my feet warm, made for relaxed and comfortable sailing. If I needed more warmth for my feet, I had a pair of lined and waterproof après-ski boots. These were much warmer than sea boots, and much easier to slip on and off. They were exclusively for wearing in the cabin; I always put on sea-boots for my rare sorties from the hatch.

The heat from my body, and the heat generated by the twice-daily use of the stove, kept the main cabin comfortably warm. The ambient temperature was about eight to ten degrees. This may seem unduly cold for a cosseted southerner, but in

High Arctic terms it verged on the tropical. Some months before leaving I had read the account of the *Fram* expedition which between 1898 and 1902 explored the northernmost Canadian islands, under the command of the extraordinary Norwegian sailor Otto Sverdrup. He and his crew survived for four years in temperatures mainly between minus forty and minus fifty degrees. On days when the thermometer rose to a mere minus twenty degrees they would strip off their shirts and play football. Everything is relative, and the human body is considerably more adaptable than we usually allow it to be.

I suspected that the cabin top and hatch configuration of *Mingming II*, somewhat different from that of *Mingming*, helped to keep the cabin warmer. The observation pod acted as a kind of heat trap. The warm air rose and collected inside the pod. On *Mingming*, the working hatch had been in this area directly overhead, and therefore allowed warm air to escape every time it was opened. On *Mingming II* I almost never opened the central hatch, set into the top of the observation pod. The working hatch was further aft, and lower down, and so its opening did not disturb the warm air trapped inside the pod. It may be too that the windows of what was almost a permanently sealed area, together with the clear hatch, allowed some heat to radiate in from the sun.

There was a serious point to all this seeking after a reliable level of warmth, dryness and comfort. It meant that I was permanently relaxed: at ease with myself and the boat. When I slept, I slept well. I was happy to take my time, as life on board was agreeable. Most importantly, though, because I was neither physically nor mentally stressed, my decision-making was of a higher quality than it may otherwise have been.

This general feeling of well-being was reinforced by the total confidence I now felt as regards *Mingming II*. We had not yet encountered anything above a Force 7, but I had spent enough time aboard her to know that she would be as good a heavy-weather boat as her predecessor. Her hull was strong, inflexible and sea kindly. She was well-balanced, light and responsive to the helm, and quick and easy to reef. The permanent boom gallows made lashing down the sail bundle an easier task than on *Mingming*. With three hatches to choose from, virtually any part of the rig was accessible without having to go on deck.

I had built *Mingming II's* interior myself, and so I felt a level of connection with it that I had never achieved on *Mingming*. The overall structural changes I had made were of a much greater order too. I had sacrificed two summers' sailing in order to create this new boat. Now I was reaping a just reward. All the singular, quirky, custom-built oddities that I had dreamed up and constructed combined to produce a satisfying and effective whole. There are millions of yachts on this planet, and not one of them resembled *Mingming II*. She was my own little practical work of art, a distillation of a lifetime's thinking, a poke in the eye of bland industrialised cloning, a statement of revolt against the conventional and the unimaginative, a celebration of whim and fancy, a phallic finger raised to establishments, busybodies, killjoys, jobsworths, bores, dolts and dullards. She expressed my yearning for unconstrained freedom. She symbolised a revulsion against the deadening hand of herding and homogenisation.

She did all this, and she sailed like a witch too. Few things could have made me happier.

Two Seals Investigate Us.

34

The breeze came and went; the fog came and went. We
stopped; we started. Hopen and Edgeøya hung on their
respective horizons, sometimes clear, sometimes mist-bound.
When the breeze came it was a fickle, contrary thing. I tacked
east and tacked west, working slowly south and keeping
well clear of the land to port and starboard. I watched out
for walruses, as we were just a few miles from the scene of
our only encounter, but none showed up. Two seals, more
coarsely headed than the sleek harp seals of Kongsøya, raised
my hopes for a moment. They slunk along in line astern,
these two, undulating along the surface and casting glances
our way. They circled us at a respectful distance and quietly
disappeared.

The persistent calms had smoothed the sea to a translucent
blue and I stared down into it. Here were whole legions
of little things getting on with their lives. Thousands of
delicate jellyfish were drifting by just a few inches below the

surface. They were tiny, these jellyfish, and perfectly formed. They were an understated and transparent bluey-grey, an exquisitely subtle colour that in a cruder form might adorn the front doors of middle-class aspirants of the wealthier London suburbs. This was a shade somehow created by nature itself, infinitely less attainable than anything man-made, and was set off by the pale white spokes that emanated in perfect symmetry from the centre of each jellyfish's back. There was something dreamlike about their coloration and their progress. They moved with the silent elegance of hot air balloons: aloft, defying gravity, but without the least apparent effort. Sometimes they drew themselves up into an inverted tulip shape, other times they relaxed to a flat mushroom. It was hard not to assign a level of intelligence to these organisms: a wise man might strive for decades to achieve their unhurried ease.

Other, much stranger, creatures occupied the next stratum down, about a foot beneath the surface. These fellows were like translucent ghosts. A globular head lead to a body like an inverted flame, both in shape and colour, to the extent of being orange at the tip. They had flame-shaped arms too, long, pointed and completely transparent. They hung vertically in the water, these chaps, maintaining their orientation with rapid movements of their arms and tail. I had never seen anything like it before, and so fished one out with my kiddies' fishing net and introduced him to life in a bucket of seawater. He was not happy. For a while he curled up into a tight ball and sulked. Then he went exploring, round and round the side of the bucket, no doubt searching for the open ocean and a star to steer by. Up close he was the most extraordinary creature, scarcely more than an inch and a half tall. His flesh was transparent, and so all his inner workings were completely visible. The inner part of his head was an array of bright orange spheres, six in all. A short gullet lead down to an oval collection of dark brown guts. That was all. The transparent flesh must have had some sort of musculature, or at least some capacity for transmitting and executing motor commands, but nothing was visible. Although the flesh looked relatively solid when the fellow was swimming, it collapsed into a shapeless glob in the bottom of the net. I photographed him and filmed him and sketched him[1]. He seemed un-mollified by all this attention, so I gently returned him to the sea.

Lower down there were more squidgy, see-through things: salps this time, tubular pumps drifting along extracting unlikely nutrients from the seawater. I had never seen them so far north before. Perhaps these were the hardier survivors, swept up into the Barents Sea by the Gulf Stream, and still going strong.

Even here, then, every cubic foot of water held its measure of living things. An extrapolation of this sample across the squillions of cubic feet of all the planet's oceans reinforced once more the notion that the sea is still the cradle of life; that, by comparison, life on the land is no more than a superficial layering. Terrestrial life clothes a minor portion of the earth's surface, giving it a limited width, but it has no depth either. It is relatively one-dimensional, existing in a single horizontal plane. If this plane sank beneath the sea, life would still flourish; conversely, a planet without the oceans would be a shrivelled, desiccated desert.

I thought about a world covered in nothing but ocean. What a strange and wonderful symmetry the planet would have. A globe of pure blue ocean, untainted by the least rocky protuberance. Perhaps, somewhere, such a world exists; probability would argue for it. And what a reinvention of life would go with it: sea-birds, amphibians, all the myriad

---

1   Kindly identified by Dr Chris Gallienne, of the Plymouth Marine Laboratory, as *Clione limacina,* or sea angel.

organisms that inhabit the margins between sea and land, all re-engineered over aeons to adapt to a new world: flying fish become sea eagles; seals become flying fish.

My reverie was interrupted by a hint of a breeze from the south-west. It was the faintest of breaths, so insubstantial that neither a cat's paw nor the least ripple marred the mirrored surface of the sea. I could feel it on my cheek, though, and for some reason it felt like a sailing wind. I hauled up all seven panels of the sail and settled us down, close-hauled on starboard tack. *Mingming II's* sail had already shown its worth, but now it excelled. *Mingming II* heeled slightly to leeward and bounded forward, cutting through the glass of the sea with a steady hiss. Her quarter wave sent out an expanding V of ripples astern. It was a kind of magic: we were advancing through a calm sea and almost motionless air at three knots or so. It was hard to figure out the mechanics of this movement. Somehow a ton of boat was being pulled to windward on the stillest of days. I suspected that for some reason the wind sheer was exaggerated; that at twenty or twenty five feet above the surface, high enough to leave the sea unruffled but low enough to catch the upper panels of the sail, the breeze was blowing much more strongly than is usual in calm conditions. Whatever the cause, the result was spectacular: perpetual motion without any discernible prime mover. My heart swelled at the joy of it; my little boat, cobbled together in a dusty boatyard, an agglomeration of off-beat whims, slicing purposefully through the Arctic seas in scarcely a breath of wind. I knew that such perfection could not last for long; it never does. Nonetheless, the unlikelihood of our progress and the sensuousness of our creaming motion combined to give a moment of total fulfilment. Of the many ways in which a man can stumble towards oblivion, this seemed one of the more agreeable.

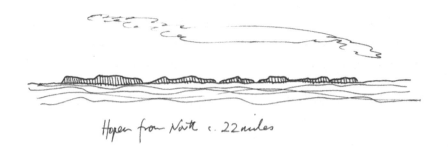

Hopen from North c. 22 miles

35

For three days we worked our way south through these stuttering winds. With the slant of the breeze predominantly from the south west, my hopes of heading towards the Sorkapp, Spitsbergen's southern cape, were quietly crushed. We had already passed that cape's latitude, and with time pushing on, I knew I would not want to turn north again should conditions allow.

My mind was now set on crossing the Greenland Sea to Jan Mayen. Three years earlier, persistent south-westerlies had put paid to a similar plan. This time round I was determined to force a course to the west, come what may. The sooner I could make my westing, the better. The further west we sailed, the less we would have to fight the north-going North Atlantic Current. We may even get some help from the East Greenland and Jan Mayen Currents. The more quickly Jan Mayen could be converted from a huge diversion to an almost straight-line point on the journey home, the less the chances that I would be discouraged should we face adverse conditions. I decided, therefore, that once we were well clear of the southern end of Spitsbergen I would tack west and keep going, even if initially we were forced a little to the north.

On the afternoon of Wednesday the sixth of August, our thirty-fourth day at sea, I noticed that the forward lashing of the top batten had partly loosened itself. I had worked hard, when designing and building the arrangement for holding in the forward ends of the battens, to end up with something totally failsafe. Seventeen hundred miles of sailing had uncovered a weakness in the design. I dropped and lashed the sail, and using the fore-hatch, examined the lashing. It would hold for little while longer, but needed to be redone and improved. For the moment there was too much of a swell to exit the hatch and make the repair; I would do it during the next flat calm.

All day the weather had been closing in, and at eleven that evening a little breeze started up from the north-east. It was a new and different wind, this one, cold and purposeful, and by two-thirty the next morning we were down to just two panels and racing to the south-south-west. For the time being I kept the wind on the port quarter, to give us our final margin of clearance from the islands of Svalbard. Later I would gybe to starboard and head west.

By six in the morning we were down to one panel, and by eight I had reduced this to just a half, a shallow triangle, enough to keep us moving well and in balance. Overnight we had passed 76°North, reinforcing my feeling that for this summer at least, that latitude marked the southern limit of the Arctic High. We were now over the shallow waters of the Spitsbergen Banks, and right on cue a fishing boat passed astern, heading west. Our days of total solitude and gentle weather were over.

We were heading back towards open sea, so gone too were the rigours of engineless pilotage around and close to the islands. This kind of navigation is a constant question of placement. If I put the boat here, or here, or here, what might be the effect of a becalming, or of an inshore current, or of an adverse tide, or of a nasty blow? Every move is circumscribed by its yet unseen consequences. It is a form of geometric chess. All possible courses are considered, then discarded one by one until the move that carries the best risk/reward ratio is arrived at. In these high latitudes in particular, no forward planning can be made on the basis of the wind of the moment: within twelve hours it will almost certainly be gone. The assumption has to be that everything will soon change. Alertness to the possible consequences of any sort of transformation must therefore be built into the pilotage process, along with an unreserved willingness to keep altering the tactics and the strategy. Yesterday's easy target may be unattainable today. No matter: rethink the plan. It is enjoyable to develop the mental fluidity that this kind of sailing requires: the constant revision of what may or may not be possible. It is this permanent uncertainty that keeps a voyage alive and interesting. The engineless sailor cannot fire up a motor to override the consequences of an error or adverse conditions; he cannot use horsepower to force a plan into conformity.

To learn willingness constantly to revise strategy, to remain always open to all possibilities, helps one along the road to what I would consider the most important attribute of the seasoned sailor: total equanimity and indifference as to what the weather brings. There is nothing to be gained from hoping for this wind or that, or from raging against headwinds or calms. You will get what you will get, sometimes helpful, sometimes unhelpful. It is healthier and less stressful to purge oneself of all hope as regards the weather, and to accept whatever comes with an equally positive mind-set. Weather is neither good nor bad; it just is. The sailor's task is to exercise his skill in all conditions without any emotional overlay. To be constantly cursing an adverse wind is a sign of navigational immaturity. Over time, all the vicissitudes of the weather even themselves out. A fair wind is pleasing, yes, but sooner or later it will be counterbalanced by its opposite. Better, then, not to rejoice in it too much, but simply to get on with the task of making the most of it. If one can accept all weather equally, sailing becomes a much calmer and more enjoyable experience. It becomes a continuous and equanimous exercise in technical ability, rather than a roller-coaster of highs and lows. This even-mindedness depends largely on confidence in one's boat and one's skill; all three aspects tend to develop together, as they are closely inter-related. Strong emotional reactions betray a lack of confidence, either in oneself or one's vessel.

The most effective destroyer of enjoyment is anxiety. To find something pleasurable is to alleviate anxiety. There is something to enjoy in all weathers. The trick is first to find it, then to concentrate on it. Emotional distancing is required; so too is a recalibration of the normal measures of comfort. Comfort is in any case a relative concept, much distorted in our over-cosseted world.

Racing downwind over the Spitsbergen Banks I thought about it a little more, and concluded that the other enemy of relaxed sailing is a misconceived notion of time, or more precisely, the relationship between past, present and future. If the past is no more than a mental construct of our experience, and the future a mental construct of our pre-supposed experience, that might imply that the only reality is the present, and it is there that we live. Yet the present moment is ungraspable. As soon as you reach out for it, it is gone. However infinitesimally you divided time, you would never arrive at the precise instant that could be deemed the present. The present is an illusion; it is no more than a chimerical interface between what we think has been and what we suppose might be. In its approximate form it is all, though, that we have. To have one's focus drawn too widely from the fleeting present is to give oneself over to wish and expectation, with their necessary corollaries: uncertainty, anxiety and fear.

These emotions, which can gnaw away at a sailor in so many ways, destroying pleasure and good decision-making, stem from over-absorption in what we suppose might be. Clearly one has to analyse the possibilities, and make the best dispositions possible, but beyond that there is nothing to be gained by worrying. The worst that can happen is that one can die. So what? It is going to happen sooner or later, and in relation to the infinite time passed peacefully before birth, and the infinite time to be passed peacefully after death, a few months or years are of little relevance. It does no harm to a sailor, or indeed any man, to learn indifference towards death.

Teal Blue Ship

36

It was a mean-hearted north-easterly that carried us out into the Greenland Sea, a cold, gimlet-eyed wind blowing straight off Franz Josef Land. It was as inconstant as it was unfriendly, this wind, sometimes working itself up into thudding gusts, sometimes whimpering to nothing. It came in, now from here, now from there, and kept me forever at the hatch, raising sail, lowering sail, easing the mainsheet, taking up the mainsheet, constantly adjusting the balance of the self-steering gear and the tiller. It made me earn my keep and I was glad of it: this was an Arctic wind if ever there was and so, for all its inconsistencies, it was the noblest of winds.

We jinked around the shallowest section of the Spitsbergen Banks, gybing first south, then west, and crossed into the Greenland Sea about thirty miles north of Bjørnøya. The frigid, lovable wind kept the tips of my fingers white with cold, but no matter, we were making our westing, heading straight for Hochstetter Bay in the far north-east of Greenland. I was happy to hold this course until stopped by land, or ice, or until the wind shifted. Technically we were crossing what the Norwegians call the Fram Strait, the stretch of water that separates Svalbard and Greenland. To make a tenuous connection with that great ship, while driven on by this polar wind, warmed me to the core. I knew well enough that my own excursions into these northern waters were little more than a pretence, a conceit, in comparison with those of the real Arctic explorers. I was little more than a tourist, a day-tripper, playing the hard man in a world become soft. I was contributing to nothing except my own sense of fulfilment, somehow trying to reconcile nineteenth century dreams with a twenty-first century world. I was profoundly aware of this sense of anachronism, and of the total inutility of what I was up to. Nonetheless, I could not see what else I could do. A whole life had driven me inexorably to this point; seeds sewn innocently sixty years previously were now bringing their final fruit. A man cannot fight his own nature.

For a while I thought that this new wind, for all its alternating between the muscular and the effete, was going to develop into something steady: a blow that would take us well on our way to the other side of the Greenland Sea. I thought that perhaps the days of calm were now behind us, but it was a premature assessment. On the afternoon of Friday the eighth of August, our thirty-fifth day at sea, and after a noon-to-noon run of eighty-one nautical miles, the breeze once more started to dwindle. I made a rare mandatory exit of the hatch to put a safety lashing on the fittings that secured the mainsheet blocks to the after rail; they looked loose and vulnerable after five weeks of hard use. By ten that evening the wind had gone. I lowered and lashed the mainsail, and on an easy sea that rolled us gently to a rhythmic lullaby, slept for eight hours. It was the longest sleep of the voyage, a deep, reviving sleep that recouped the accumulated deficit of the previous weeks of intense pilotage, the sort of sleep I would only ever allow myself in the remotest of open waters. I slept, relaxed and happy, satisfied with our little adventure around the islands of eastern Svalbard, my subconscious already ranging ahead across the Greenland Sea to that other island, Jan Mayen, and all its possibilities.

At nine the next morning a zephyr came up somewhere from the west. I raised seven panels of the sail and in the longest and oiliest of swells we ghosted painfully on, now diverted to the south-west. Within a couple of hours the puffs had spun round to the east and we were back on course. We passed by the prominent red top and dark green neck of a bottle floating upright in the sea. I had no doubt that it contained a message, but it was past us before I could fish it out. I was not disappointed: somehow I knew exactly what the message said:

Hello, my name is Olga i am beautiful dorter of rich Russian oligarch. I am stranded on island Bear island not far from were you are right now. Please come and rescue me. Love and kiss, Olga.

The prospect sounded appealing, but it gets tiresome, after a while, having wealthy young beauties forever chasing after you. I decided to give Olga a miss and sailed on.

By noon, after a day's run of just thirty-five miles, I had once more lowered and lashed the mainsail. The constant slatting was no good for the rig, and no good for my ears: I wanted to eat my sparse lunch in peace. A light breeze soon came back and I raised the sail. The wind died again and I lowered the sail. A great skua flew past and was attacked by a screaming Iceland gull. I raised the sail for fifteen minutes and gave up again. Two great black-backed gulls kept us company for a while. A small teal blue ship,

147

its name indecipherable, passed by half a mile to our west, heading south.

Overnight the breeze came up a bit more steadily, first from the north then swinging round to the east. Heavy cloud rolled in, bringing the occasional shower and brief streaks of sunshine. We moved gaily along under just three panels.

By noon the next day we had covered fifty-two miles, and the cabin felt warmer than it had for a while. This was not surprising: we were now almost at 74°North, three hundred miles south of our highest latitude. It was probable, too, that we were now crossing the mid-point of the warmer North Atlantic Current.

An hour after midday a disgracefully sleek fishing boat appeared off our starboard quarter, heading our way and angling in towards us. It was huge, with a cruise-liner bridge and bristling with electronic gadgetry It was clearly designed to extract as much life from the ocean as possible with the minimum of human involvement. In the lively sea that was running, the only name I could read on the ship's side was the word *Klaksvik*. The fishing boat overhauled us, about a quarter of a mile on our starboard beam, and I decided to be sociable. I assembled my hand-held VHF radio and called up the ship. I had not spoken to anyone for thirty-eight days and so was looking forward to a nice matey chinwag, an old-sea-dogs-exchanging-yarns-of-the-Far-North moment. It was not to be. The skipper of the *Gadus* was not a happy man. He seemed more than reasonably offended by the fact that I called him up using his port of registration rather than his ship's name. *My ship is GADUS! GADUS!* With admirable restraint I apologised for the error, and refrained from suggesting that it may be helpful if the ship's name were painted in letters considerably larger than its port, rather than vice versa, but from then on it was all downhill. I managed to extract the information that the ship was Faroese and homeward bound, but he clearly did not want to talk to me. For a while I thought that it was perhaps because I was flying a Red Ensign, or because he felt I ought not to have been there anyway. Perhaps his hold was not as full as he would have liked, or his wife had just telephoned him to say that she had changed her mind, and wasn't going to leave him after all. Then I realised the reason for his unfriendliness. He had tried to rescue Olga, and she had put him straight:

Sorry, I waiting for close-by good-breeding Englishman with very nice yacht and banking at Coutts. You go fry your smelly Faroe fish some place other...

The 'Gartus' of Klaksvik

37

The *Gadus*[2] of Klaksvik quickly disappeared over the horizon ahead and I breathed a deep sigh of relief for every innocent living creature. The *Gadus* was as good a metaphor as one could find for rapacious intelligence enhanced by advanced technology, for insouciant greed made slick with computerisation. In one sense here was nothing new: for centuries the scouring of the planet's oceanic life had been financed by rich men, the 'owners', always in search of industrial efficiencies. They owned the capital, the ships, the crews. What was impossible to understand, though, was by what logic they felt they owned too the rights to murder, for their personal profit, every marine creature that could be disembowelled and recycled for economic benefit. How could

---

2 Sharp-eyed readers will have spotted the difference in the spelling of the ship's name between the log-book sketch and the text. I interpreted the skipper's word as *Gartus*. Later research showed it to be *Gadus*.

anyone have imagined, for example, that they had a legitimate right to finance the extermination, not just of a single blue whale, but of almost the entire species? Here was a failure of morality; commercial opportunism taken to a grotesque extreme: the fact that one has the means to do something, and that it is in a narrow sense 'legal', does not necessarily mean that it is right. Jurisprudence has its limitations; the creatures of the wide oceans lie outside the concept of proprietorship; they are life, evolution, the beating heart and history of the animate world.

Force Six Seascape

38

The wind stuttered for another twenty-four hours or so, sometimes forcing us down to just two panels in bouts of squally rain, sometime leaving us languishing in a left-over swell from the north-east. For a while the sky cleared, giving the sun full licence to brighten up our dull little world.

By noon the next day we had covered seventy-four miles, and within an hour or two, with a rising breeze from the north-north-west, the weather finally found some stability. From here on, right to the Shetlands, our voyage would be defined by muscular northerlies. With the exception of one short lapse at Jan Mayen, this wind would drive us on homewards with unrelenting power.

For the moment, though, it was just a new wind, pretty much on the beam, and so was a welcome, expansive wind. At times it wound itself up to a Force 7, laced with vicious downpours and flashes of sunshine. With just one panel set we rolled joyfully on in a rising sea, now bound fair for Jan

Mayen, now firmly centred in the Greenland Sea. On we raced, with the days merging one into the other, our daily runs up to ninety miles or so. The cabin grew cooler as we left the last vestiges of the Gulf Stream astern and moved towards the icy water of the East Greenland Current.

The cloud thickened and the squalls came in more strongly. With Jan Mayen now just a couple of days' sail away, I began to consider the state of the sky with more attention; my main hope for this third visit was, after all, to get a proper view of Mount Beerenberg, and for that I needed a clear atmosphere. The prognosis was not good. The layer of lower cloud was by now so solid and seemingly immutable that I suspected that its upper side had been sanded down and epoxied to the sky above; nothing was going to budge it. It was maybe two thousand feet high, and so would have the bulk of Mount Beerenberg's seven thousand feet in its grip. I stared glumly at this expanse of cloud, clearly built with loving care to last a thousand years, and wondered how I might induce it to go away. Having dismissed incantation and prayer as so much baloney, I thought that perhaps an appropriate little dance might do the trick, but *Mingming II* was rolling around too much for that sort of caper. I decided to stick to sailoring and accept whatever came our way.

A lone puffin crossed astern, suggesting the proximity of land: Jan Mayen was now a hundred and sixty miles ahead. The heavy squalls persisted, keeping me busy at the hatch adjusting the sail. I hardened up the sheet as the wind backed to north-west. We were now plunging along at five knots or so, sailing full and by like good old-timers. A shaft of sunlight pierced the epoxy cloud and quickly withdrew. The wind veered back to its starting point and started to drop away. One by one each panel was hauled aloft. The Nordkapp of Jan Mayen was now just eighty miles away. In a lumpy sea I finally raised the seventh panel, keeping us ghosting along.

I broke out rations from the aft stowage, moving them to the forward containers. Some quick calculations showed we could keep the sea for a good while longer.

Above, the news was both good and bad. To the north the sky was clearing a little, with the solid stratus making way for a mix of blue sky and some sub-standard clouds of the *Hindenbergus arcticus* type. They lacked the scale and puffed-up glory and absolute symmetry of form of their more northern counterparts. In fact they were disappointingly shoddy imitations, but they at least broke up the cloud cover. The heavy layering of impenetrable cloud still persisted to the south and west, though, where Jan Mayen lay waiting to be discovered. On a clear day Mount Beerenberg would surely have stood white and proud above the south-west horizon. As it was I peered into the gloom and saw nothing.

The wind expired. I dropped and lashed the sail and we lay to a gentle calm just sixty-four miles from the Nordkapp. It seemed appropriate. *Mingming* had been becalmed at a similar distance during both her approaches to Jan Mayen from the south; there was no reason why her bigger sister should be spared the same rite of passage. There was something edifying about this slight pause before the final run in. It allowed a moment to contemplate the great mass that lay ahead. There are few, if any, more impressive juxtapositions of sea and land to be found on this planet; few, if any, more starkly grandiose islands. Each time we had come we had been forced to stop and reflect, while the island lay hidden just out of range. We had been held for a while in the ante-chamber, poor supplicants that we were, before finally being allowed into the Great Presence. Once more we were observing the ritual.

Yes, we were poor supplicants, pared down and threadbare, scarcely more than barefoot pilgrims with staff and begging bowl. Whether or not our visit to Jan Mayen yielded any worthwhile reward, we had covered the long track the hard way, and therefore had earned the right to be there. Once again I thought about the conflict between means and rights. A man with a healthy bank balance and time to fill before the grave might well buy an annual pilgrimage across the globe, complete with long-haul flight, many-starred accommodation, air-conditioned coach tour, adventure guide and of course a nightly performance of ethnic music and dance by the local indigenes. He joins a billion other pleasure-seekers circulating the planet in a destructive touristic frenzy. Time was when a man could refresh his spirit with a week in the Lake District. Now it's Patagonia one year, Siberia the next, the Galapagos the year after. The justification is simple: I can afford it, so who or what is to stop me? For the moment there is no barrier, except a sense of self-restraint, and a greater respect for our small world. It is not a theme park; it is a fragile living organism, and it is all we have. One day we will all have to re-learn to live happily at home.

At two-thirty on the morning of Friday, the fifteenth of August, our forty-third day at sea, a little breeze came up from the north-west. With six, and soon seven, panels set we crept in towards the island. I became doubly attentive to navigation. While becalmed we had been pushed seven miles to the south and there was a danger, in the light headwind, that we may not be able to weather the Nordkapp. Having twice sailed up the east side of Jan Mayen, I was determined this time to have a look at the west coast. I hardened up, therefore, to give us good margin of error around the island's northern tip.

By nine-thirty a section of the lower slopes of Mount Beerenberg, squeezed between sea and sky, was visible on the port bow. There was not much to see: just a few diagonal streaks of black rock grazing the horizon. The grey of the surrounding ice was scarcely distinguishable from the enveloping cloud, but some aspect of its chemistry gave it a distinct solidity and translucence. We were fifty-five miles off. Assuming that the linear section that we could see was the base of a roughly equilateral triangle, it was possible to construct a mental image of the whole mountain hidden in the cloud. It was of monstrous proportions. Had the day been clear it would have dominated the south-western sky, even at that distance.

Now that Mount Beerenberg was within our sights I felt a certain calmness. The winds were light and capricious, but we could take as much time as we liked to close the mountain, constantly alert for any revelation of its topmost slopes and, if we were lucky, its crowning cone. This was the final point of inflection of our voyage. We had ranged a fair way around the Barents Sea and the Greenland Sea, and had seen a host of wonders. Now Jan Mayen had drawn us back once again. The magnetism of the island was in proportion to its mass, the pull of its slopes irresistible. I had no idea what the next day or two would bring, as so much depended on winds and on cloud cover, but I could feel a growing sense of anticipation. I was determined to make the most of this third visit. I wanted to know the island better, to understand more fully its brutal beauty.

The wind veered a little to north-north-west, aiding our approach. A patch of clearer sky worked its way south from the northern horizon. I kept my vigil in the hatchway, eyes searching for what they might see.

first Huk of Jan Mayen from NE c. 55 miles.

39

By midday our noon-to-noon distances totalled more than two thousand three hundred and fifty miles. Bit by bit we had accumulated a reasonable voyage in our wake. One of the most pleasing aspects was that it had been done with a single sail. From a practical perspective it had been liberating to do away once and for all with any sort of headsail. With no more complex paraphernalia for raising and lowering the jib, with no more sorties to the foredeck, with no more decisions to be made as to whether to carry a headsail or not, life aboard had become simpler and more stress-free, and sail-handling had become much quicker. The bigger mainsail, with its more advanced design, had more than compensated for the lack of a headsail.

More than that, though, the sailing was more integrated and harmonious. In reducing the sail plan to its most basic form, a single sail, I had arrived at the essence of the matter. It was the inevitable end-point of a quest to achieve the maximum with the minimum, of a desire to find the simplest expression of sailing possibility. I had not foreseen the level of satisfaction that would come from voyaging under a single sail. There was something atavistic and fundamental in the pleasure it gave me. Nothing could be simpler than one sail on an un-stayed mast; this was how it had started. I felt more of a connection with the sailors of the distant past, more firmly rooted in an ancient practice. The materials I had used in the construction were of course modern, but the concept was unchanged. The rig was supple and unstressed. There was no wire, no winches. The softness of the rig and the simplicity of its handling allowed for a greater awareness of the origins of the art; I felt a kind of complicity with the men who had first ventured to sea in rudimentary sailing boats. I did not kid myself: I still had a thousand advantages over the early voyagers. I was in no way emulating them. Nonetheless, for the first time I felt that I had found a way back to at least some aspects of their frame of mind.

I had found a way back, too, to the heart of my own sailing impulse. I had finally arrived at the place I had always wanted to be: at sea in the strongest, simplest boat I could make. With this tiny yacht and its one sail I could go almost anywhere. That was the notion that had always captivated me: the boundless possibility of a sailing craft. Along with that went the conviction that the purer the conception, the greater the satisfaction. Every superfluous element that diluted that purity was a contamination of the idea. *Mingming II's* rig was now as pure as I knew how to make it. It was controlled by just four lines, all operable from the hatch. With those four lines I could do everything necessary with the sail in just a few seconds and with minimal effort.

I kept my vigil, watching for any break in the cloud heading south over Mount Beerenberg, and decided that I should not unduly congratulate myself for getting around the planet with little more than a hull, a stick, a rectangle of cloth and a litre or two of bio-ethanol. Compared to the effortless journeying of the whales and dolphins and shearwaters it was a laboured, contrived progress. I wondered whether deep down that was really what I was after: voyaging so pared down that finally I could cross the oceans as naked and unfettered as the creatures of the sea. Was that it? A desire for total liberation? A wish to have nothing but the skin of my body between myself and the consuming elements? An urge for total immersion in a world spared the stultifying contrivances of man? Was this simple voyaging an act of rebellion, a revolt against a constant imprisonment? It was only in the bleakness of these wild places that I could find clarity and repose; it was only here that my mind, the only thing that was truly mine, could find the space to soar.

I realised that a prerequisite for this freeing of the spirit was the simplest of boats; a boat that provided the least obtrusive interface between myself and the sea; a boat that could be sailed so effortlessly and so softly that it was little more than an extension of my own body, and therefore did not interfere with my task of observing and absorbing.

I saw that there was a kind of paradox here. To build and sail a boat like *Mingming II* undoubtedly required a certain level of experience and know-how; it could not be done without technical ability. The simplicity of operation was art concealing art. Whatever skill I may have applied in developing my yachts, it was only a means to an end, not an end in itself. It was almost a reverse technology: technique concealed beneath a rough exterior; science distilled almost to nothingness. The aim was to use technology in such a way as to take it out of the equation, to leave it behind and render it invisible. Only in this way could I liberate myself.

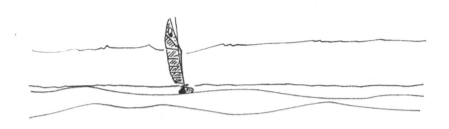

40

The long and narrow break in the cloud moved on south and slowly revealed an upper cross-section of the mountain. A huge shoulder of ice projected out in our direction, glistening in the low sunlight. On each side, to the north and south, stretched swathes of steep black rock. I had not expected this; my mental image had always been of a cone of pure white. Below the cloud layer, still in murky shadow, I could make out the two nearest extremities of the mountain's base, the Nordkapp and the Nordaustkapp, and so could start to get a sense of the whole. We were still fifty miles off, and could only see a lower and a middle strip, but it was already heart-stopping in its proportions.

With the cloud structure and light constantly changing I took a series of photographs, hoping to catch the definitive image. At that distance there was little chance of success, but I persevered. My official duties as Founder, President, and indeed the only Fully Paid-up Member of the Distant

Glacier Photographic Society, weighed heavily upon me. I remembered all the glaciers which had taunted me above a far horizon:

Oraefajökull, southern Iceland: sixty miles
Drangajökull, north-west Iceland: forty miles
Snaefellsjökull: west Iceland: forty-five miles
Edgeøyajokulen: east Svalbard: thirty-five miles.

Few men have laboured so hard to capture such a catalogue of fuzzy images of high ice drowned in cloud.

I kept at it, though, for two reasons. Firstly, experience had taught me that once home, with editing software and a computer screen to help, it is possible to find detail that is simply not visible at the time of photographing. The memory, too, is unreliable; even poor images are a good aid to recall. More importantly, though, I kept at it because there was always a possibility, with the broken cloud moving across, that Mount Beerenberg's crater might be revealed, if only for a few seconds. If it were, I wanted to capture the moment. This would be, in both senses, the pinnacle of my career as a Photographer of Distant Glaciers. Should I succeed, there was a good chance that an article, written by my own hand and illustrated with my own photographs, may find its way into the Society Newsletter, of which I happened to be Editor. It was an opportunity I could not miss.

The line of cloud that was hiding the topmost portion of the mountain crept higher, revealing more rock streaked vertically with couloirs of ice. The northern ridge showed one or two jagged shoulders of rock subsiding into ice-filled saddles. Here and there the ice burned a blinding white where caught by a shaft of sunlight. The upper cloud was still thinning, breaking into fluffy horizontal wisps. I could not be sure whether it was close to the crater or not.

A corner of the cloud lifted further, showing another bulge on the northern slope. At first I thought my eyes were deceiving me, but a hard look with the binoculars confirmed my impression: to the south of this bulge the rock levelled off almost horizontally. The cloud lifted just a few metres further, creating the narrowest strip of hazy blue right across the top of the mountain. Here, at last, was the crater fully revealed. It was much wider than I had anticipated; perhaps our distance from the mountain was still distorting the overall proportions. The play of the light created an extraordinary juxtaposition between the mountain's base, black and hardly visible in the thick murk at sea level, the upper edge of the cloud layer, now brilliant white in the sunshine, and above that, in a sort of halo around Mount Beerenberg's crater, a mix of ethereal cloud and pale blue sky. A religious man may have extracted some symbolism from this progression from black earth to light-filled heavens. For me it was no more than a happy confluence of circumstance. It did accentuate, though, the grandeur and loftiness of this peak which I had been seeking for so long.

The crater was soon lost behind the cloud. I felt a kind of calm, a feeling of completeness. Yes, it was only a ridge of jagged and hostile rock hoisted high into the Arctic air, but it had worked away at me like a persistent itch. The itch was now soothed away. I had seen the elusive peak of Mount Beerenberg from the deck of my own little yacht. I had a sense of its scale and form. My imaginings had at last been replaced by a real image.

There remained just one aspiration: to see the whole mountain uncovered from top to bottom. I had now seen almost all its component parts, but as vast pieces of a confused jigsaw puzzle. I had little doubt that the whole would be much, much greater than the sum of those individual parts. I knew, though, that the chances of seeing the mountain clear from water's edge to crater were slim. The cloud was thickening once again, tempering any wishful thinking.

At five that afternoon I discovered that my main camcorder had stopped working. Nothing I did would induce it to switch on. It was the same camera which had malfunctioned after being doused with sea spray off north-west Iceland a few years earlier. Since then I had always taken two camcorders aboard, and spread the filming between the two as a safety measure. Nonetheless, most of the important sequences of the voyage so far, such as our close encounter with the humpback whales off Kongsøya, had been recorded on the main camera. These moments were irreplaceable, but there was nothing I could do except hope that eventually the camcorder's data would be retrievable from its hard drive. [3]

In a patchy wind and heavier, moisture-laden air we kept on due west to position ourselves ten miles or so to the north of the Nordkapp. I heaved to and slept for a while. The mist closed in further. We were now just above 71°North, and so the Arctic nights were becoming gloomy. I hung off the north end of the island, with nothing of it visible, and waited for some stronger light. It was a familiar story: most of our island landfalls on this voyage had followed a similar sequence. At two in the morning a series of heavy rain squalls passed through; by five-thirty we were submerged in a pall of thick mist. Just one thing was in our favour: the wind had backed to north-east, giving an ideal following wind for running down the west side of Jan Mayen. There was nothing to be gained by waiting any longer. I put us about and headed south towards the Nordkapp.

---

3   Eventually a specialist engineer from the Midlands managed to recover the data. In payment I let him have the camcorder for spare parts; after 20,000 miles at sea and two malfunctions it could no longer be trusted.

41

It was an act of faith, to sail through the choking gloom towards the foot of that great volcano. I could see nothing, and so had to trust to instinct and the steepness of the cliffs' descent into the sea to keep us out of trouble. In the abysmal light and visibility I could not reasonably expect any reward from even a close pass of Mount Beerenberg's base. It had to be done, though. If I held off we would go home empty-handed. By forcing our way in there was always a chance that something worthwhile might eventuate; it would at least slant the low probability slightly in our favour.

After an hour the mist thinned a little. The cloud base was still low, perhaps at three or four hundred feet, but between this layer and the sea the black presence of Mount Beerenberg insinuated itself into the grey directly ahead. Two almost vertical strips of dirty pewter broke the uniform blackness of the cliffs: the two main features on this north-west side, the Kjerulf and Weyprecht glaciers. They fall from vertiginous heights, these two, and still have tongues projecting a little way into the sea.

To have them in my sights galvanised my resolve. This was almost certainly the last big moment of the voyage. The weather was grim but the wind was fair, now blowing with a reassuring consistency on the port quarter. There was no guarantee that I would ever be here again, that I would have another chance to feel the scent and breath and power of this sleeping giant. I disconnected the self-steering gear and, sitting comfortably on my low bridge deck seat in the hatchway, took over the steering with the steering lines. This was a personal matter now. I was going to sail in as close as I dared to the bigger of the two glaciers, the Weyprecht. For that I needed to have *Mingming II* under my direct control, firstly so that I could sense immediately any change in the conditions, secondly because that was how it had to be: one small man helming one small boat to the very foot of the mountain.

The cloud lifted a little further. Ahead there were some small breaks in the cover: a few shafts of sunlight pierced through, transforming the upper slopes of the glaciers from dirty grey to sparkling white. The uniform black of the cliffs took on shape and light and shadow. Now three-dimensional, the sides of the mountain revealed their great shoulders riven with deep declivities. We were still a good two hours' sail away, but I was fixated by the scale and strange beauty of the scene: sombre precipices disappearing skywards, cut vertically with glistening rivers of ice.

The play of sunlight on the glaciers raised my hopes: perhaps we would have a good day after all. I had been staring ahead for an hour, imprinting every detail of the scene on my memory, and calculating the best line of approach for our final run in. The need to check the whole horizon finally asserted itself. I looked astern and groaned. Bearing down on us was a mass of impenetrable cloud reaching right down to sea level.

The mist from astern soon had us in its clutches, closing out the land once more, and squashing my raised expectations. The heavy cloud drained the world of all but the most minimal light; the day was regressing rather than advancing. I kept on, now steering by compass, and searched the sky for any hint of a change. After an hour the mist started to thin a little and the long spit of the Nordkapp, now on our port beam, showed through the gloom.

The light was abysmal, the visibility poor, and for a while it all seemed hopeless; the chances of getting in close and having a good look at the base of the mountain were slim. I thought about things a little more. My three voyages encompassing Jan Mayen totalled the best part of ten thousand miles of sailing. We were now within five miles of the Weyprecht Glacier. The wind was ideal. I simply could not let the opportunity pass. Even in bad light, if I could sail in close enough, I could surely capture some good images. Frustration overcame navigational defensiveness. If there was any moment to take a risk, this was it. There was only one thing to do: to stand in and keep standing in, much closer than I had originally intended; to keep on until I could almost stroke the glacier and feel its coolness.

Doubly resolved, I took up the task again. The breeze was freshening, and with just three panels set we skipped easily along in a following swell. It was my one hope, this wind. It was blowing directly along the line of the cliffs, and so would minimise the two things that most concerned me: sudden violent squalls coming in from anywhere, and dead, windless patches. These are the usual fare when sailing under high Arctic cliffs, and for the engineless sailor they can be a nightmare. Many are the hours I have spent hobby-horsing helplessly under the heights of the Nordaustkapp on the east side of Mount Beerenberg. The prospect of repeating that within a stone's throw of the Weyprecht Glacier was not enticing, but I had confidence in the feel of the wind. Despite my determination to sail in as close as I could, I knew well enough that should I detect any hint of awkwardness in the breeze I would not be slow to retreat. Any rashness would still be moderated by a strong sense of survival.

With the wind still on the port quarter we were angling in to the cliffs and the glacier. The mist cleared a little and so I could once again steer visually, but nothing on this day was going to be easy: just before eleven in the morning a squall of torrential rain once more blotted out the base of the mountain. Rather than head in blind, I gybed and heaved to on starboard tack. In the changeable conditions this new bout of thick weather was unlikely to last long, but I decided that if it did, I would stand off and on until there was an improvement. The priority was to keep to windward of the glacier until I could be sure of a good pass.

The rain cleared, the light improved marginally, and I resumed the tangential run in to the Weyprecht Glacier. I raised another panel of sail, to give more power should we need to make a hasty retreat. The wind held steady. We closed the sheer wall of rock stretching away to north and south, and rising uncapped into the cloud above. I was now firmly out of my navigational comfort zone. To give the approach some structure, and to enable me to make a regular formal assessment of whether to advance or withdraw, I broke our progress down into blocks of time. At first each block was fifteen minutes. I resolved to sail on for fifteen minutes, then, if there were no change to the conditions, I started another fifteen minute period, and so on. Somehow this mechanism gave me the courage to keep sailing further and further in.

The time came when fifteen minutes was too long to stomach, and so I reduced the final run in to blocks of five minutes. I forced us on: *just five minutes more.* We were sailing into the end of the world: the cliffs soared skywards almost overhead and blocked the whole eastern horizon. Now that we were so close I could see all the subtle detail of their shape and coloration. The rock was not black; it was a deep chocolate brown and tinged on its exposed curves and corrugations with the startling lime-green tint of the lichen growing there. It was an extraordinarily sumptuous combination of colour: a dark, rich brown lifted by a sheen of fruity green. The rock seemed to glow. There was something medieval about the palette: I could envisage a lady in a tower enfolded in stuff of this gorgeous brown edged with lemon-green.

Just five more minutes. We sailed on, and now I could see streams of melt-water tumbling down almost vertical gullies. Everything was unashamedly precipitous. We were heading for the midpoint of a mountainside: above, it rose seven thousand feet to the edge of the crater; below, it fell away another four thousand feet to the depths of the Norwegian Sea. Now I could see patches of reddish rock infused into the brown. Whether this was caused by a different type of lichen, or whether it was oxidisation of the rock itself was impossible to determine. Later that day, further south, we would see whole buttresses the colour of autumnal leaves.

Another five minutes. It was the glacier itself that now had my whole attention. We were now dizzyingly close, and it was not at all as I had expected. This was not the smooth-topped ice of Edgeøya's Stonebreen. From its highest point, where it plunged down through the cloud, to the short hook projecting into the sea, the glacier was a riot of anarchic sculpture. Armies of demented elves had been let loose on it with picks and shovels and had gauged out a million narrow and intersecting trenches. They were deep, these crisscrossing wounds in the ice, and between them were left standing thousands of pillars of ice; tiny towers, close-packed and dishevelled.

The wind blew up more strongly, perhaps through a funnelling effect, and I reduced sail to two panels.

Just five minutes more. I kept on in, tingling with a delicious terror. The Weyprecht is not a wide glacier, perhaps quarter of a mile, and it now took up my whole field of view. The rock that framed it was now a vertical cliff that seemed to lean forward over my head. Only the narrowest stretch of water remained; we were almost subsumed into the rock and ice.

Crowds of fulmars wheeled around, giving the only hint of normality to the scene. Otherwise, it was another planet. The glacier defied adequate description. Here was a cascade of ice that was pitted, fissured, scoured, deformed, twisted, chiselled and riven. Thousands of tiny pinnacles crowded together, a jumble of spiky crenellations. It was a monstrous bed of icy nails for a lumbering northern troll.

In parts the ice glowed blue-white with a beauty all at odds with its deranged architecture. It had not arrived unscathed from its slow descent of the mountainside. The edges, where the ice had forced its way down its moraine, were black with the rock, gravel, dirt and general detritus picked up and absorbed during the journey seawards. The surface, too, was scarred with mucky patches that added to the general air of dissolution.

Five minutes was up and now my nerve was failing. I could see the waves washing at the glacier's foot. I had lost all sense of scale and distance. I had no idea whether I was a hundred yards off or five hundred. All I knew was that I was staring at the seaward end of the glacier almost eyeball to eyeball. I could make out every nuance of its texture and colour. The tongue met the sea with a low and uneven vertical face. Across this face ran a thin blackish stripe, caused perhaps by some long-ago deposit of volcanic ash. Time had destroyed the regularity of the glacier and so the stripe was now a crooked up-and-down affair, which at the south end of the low ice-cliff disappeared into the sea at an acute angle. This simply reflected the chaotic geometry of the whole icy agglomeration. It was all one great mess; it was falling to bits. It was still there, though, a gargantuan frozen tongue licking the sea at just 71°North, a last vestige of the Ice Age.

Another five minutes would have had us hard against the ice. I had abandoned so much habitual caution, and was by now so profoundly happy to be right there, at that outlandish spot, overwhelmed by the gorgeous insanity of the scene and our tenuous participation in it, that it would have been easy to sail on; not for five minutes, but for another three or four, enough to put paid to the tiny strip of sea that still lay between us and the glacier, enough to leave well astern all those cloying notions of good sense that make us such whimpering, hollow men. I could have sailed on and attempted one moment of glorious abandon. I could have sailed on and lanced a jet of saliva at the ice, not to show contempt, but to leave there one intimate trace of myself. I could have sailed on and watched the shadow of *Mingming II's* sail pass along the glacier's tongue; brief, spectral, wholly misplaced.

Yes, had I been a real man I would have crossed those remaining yards to the very threshold of that strange wilderness, but sense, supposedly good, held me back; I could not do it. I gybed and eased the mainsheet to run to the south-west, parallel with the ramparts of brown and green.

The Kvalrossen from SW c. 6 miles

42

Jan Mayen. Once more the island had me totally in her grip. All I could see, in the low cloud scudding through, was a shifting approximation of the western coastline: the great base of Mount Beerenberg easing down to the rounded central hills, a curve of low mountains rising to the southern peaks. It was a wild and stirring sight, enhanced by the swish and roll of *Mingming II* as she raced joyfully on in a white-topped sea.

In our wake was a string of untamed islands, all of them, except Abeløya, lofty and overpowering. We had seen towering headlands and glaciers stretching to the horizon, black cliffs and imperious buttresses, walls of ice and the great gauges of empty moraines; astern was a whole catalogue of Arctic topography. Nothing, though, equalled Jan Mayen. This was the queen of islands: the most beautiful and varied, the most outrageous. Here was the most sublime expression of unimaginable forces sculpting the crust of the earth. It would have been so easy for the great cone of Mount Beerenberg to have skewed the balance of the island, to have weighted it too much to the north, but the long string of mountains to the south, although much lower, provided the necessary lever to bring the whole back into an unlikely harmony. The centre of gravity of the island was at its low central waist, where it ought to be, providing the perfectly placed fulcrum between the opposing masses to the north and south.

Overlaying this natural balance was the extraordinary variety in the shape and character of the hills and mountains, and of the island's coastline. Here were smooth cones of every size, jagged ridges, misshapen headlands, tight horseshoe bays encased in cliff, beaches of black volcanic shingle, slopes that had collapsed into the sea, leaving gaping rents of crumbling rock. There was no end to the variations on the theme of the interaction between earth, ice, sea and relentless weather.

We sped south, still hugging Mount Beerenberg's base. The tumbling remnants of volcanic rock were now less steep. Gullies and hollows were pitted with ice; some patches seemed suspended almost vertically. Fissures in the rock, cutting across at indiscriminate angles, sectioned the green powdering into a patchwork of crazy paving.

The cloud started to rise, uncovering on Mount Beerenberg's upper slopes a field of ice broken only by the occasional rocky hummock and steeper section of cliff. It was totally unexpected, this sudden lift in the cloud base, and my blood coursed a little faster. A tiny rent in the cloud revealed a streak of blue. I watched closely and realised what was happening. The mountain itself was breaking up the cloud pouring across it from the north, throwing it into a confused and disconnected jumble. Bigger patches of clear sky came and went, and to the south of the hidden crater the overall cloud base moved slowly higher.

I had witnessed this slow undressing of Jan Mayen on previous voyages, and knew how seductive and frustrating it could be: an ankle or shoulder here, perhaps over there a hint of upper thigh glimpsed through diaphanous cloud. Jan Mayen was coy about her physical charms, but knew how to tease; I had no expectation that she would cast off the final veil. I watched, though, sad punter that I was, eager for the least titivation.

On we swept, our fulmar escort now in the hundreds, adding to the movement and effervescence of the day. Ahead the cloud lifted and thinned, so that the whole of the west coast was now clearly defined. It was the reverse side of the coin I knew so well after two passages up the east coast. The general lay-out and outline of the hills and mountains was instantly recognisable, but in a dislocated way. Everything had switched: our previous light south-westerlies were now a beefy north-easterly; the cloud cover was darker, more confused, more imposing; the coastline here was starker, more detailed, with several prominent headlands and protruding razorbacks of rock; and this time we were heading south, at the end of a voyage, homeward bound.

One of the headlands stood out in dark relief against the cloud behind and on its seaward end was perched a church. It was tall and rectangular, with a short steeple, the kind of thing that Irish monks of the middle ages might have erected to house their penitence. This impression was aided by the absurdity of its location. I could find no reference to a building on the chart. In fact it was no more than a grand *trompe l'oeuil* hewn by nature out of the rock itself. It was only an hour or two later, when viewed from the south-west, that the illusion dissolved.

The cloud continued to lift over Mount Beerenberg. From time to time the sun shone through to the south of the crater, setting what were now pristine fields of ice alight. Higher up, shoulders of rock began to appear where the cone steepened towards its apex. For the first time I could see almost the whole mountain; only the uppermost segment was still veiled by cloud.

The volcano was numbing in its scale. Here was the molten core of the earth relocated to the atmosphere; countless trillions of tonnes of lava spewed skywards. How many millions of years had it taken before the crater first broached the surface of the sea? How long had it then taken for the crater to lift itself seven thousand feet into the sky by this colossal act of levitation? Was the process finished? Might the ice-fields once more sizzle and steam under white-hot lava?

I reminded myself that the land is neither fixed nor stable. Its solidity is an illusion fed by the brevity of our life-span. It comes and goes.

The cloud was now hiding only the very top of the crater. It would lift no higher. Nonetheless, almost the whole cone was uncovered, and to complete the picture I only had to add the image of the topmost ridge imprinted on my memory the day before.

It was enough. I had sailed here three times and now I could take the mountain home. I had seen the island laid out from end to end in one almost unblemished panorama. It was much more than I had anticipated just a few hours earlier.

The south-western skirt of Mount Beerenberg curved away to the east, putting us into more open water and encouraging a fresher breeze. We rolled across the wide bay that indents Jan Mayen's western coast, and headed for a sharp projection of rock, the Kvalrossen, at the bay's southern extremity. We were soon level with the ecclesiastical headland, and I fancied I could hear the distant drone of plainsong and the slap of sandals on stone-cold flags. Behind the cape stretched the soft, more modulated curves of the central hills, homely hummocks beside the great cone to the north.

I angled in towards the Kvalrossen, as I wanted to make a fairly close pass. Behind this sheltering razorback, and encircled by a tight ring of high slopes, was one of Jan Mayen's better anchorages I wanted to have a look in. Perhaps there would be a boat in there.

The Kvalrossen is a distinctive outcrop of sheer black rock, hump-shaped, with a separate pinnacle rising from the low spit at its seaward end. As we passed by I studied it from every angle but could not quite reconcile its form with its name – the Walrus. Perhaps it looked different from the shore. Perhaps, at a low spring tide, it might have looked like a very fat walrus lying on its back, tusks in the air. Maybe my one encounter with walruses did not qualify me to make the judgement anyway.

It marked the entrance to what was clearly a snug pace to lie, in all but westerly weather: a horse-shoe of protective but climbable lime-green slopes. The anchorage was empty and I was glad of it: this was a day to have Jan Mayen to myself. There were of course huts on the island housing a transitory team of scientists, but they were out of view and out of mind.

We raced on. Astern the view had resolved itself into a masterly composition: cutting across the foreground the black and hard-edged silhouette of the Kvalrossen; in the middle ground the headland with its putative chapel, now grainy and dreamlike as it merged into the cliff below; to the east the undulating contours of the island's waist; and dominating the whole, the icy brooding presence of Mount Beerenberg, its upper third now lost in a blanket of thick cloud.

The mountains of the south, now on our port beam, were similarly veiled, and so all that was visible were their lower slopes. These mirrored their counterparts on the eastern side; in many places the rock had slid away to form abrupt cliffs; here and there now-defunct glaciers had bulldozed broad highways to the sea. The only difference was the colour, for these slopes glowed green, in contrast to their grey eastern counterparts. It took me a while to find an explanation: I was there much later in the summer than on my two previous visits. The growing season was now at its zenith. With the upper peaks hidden the overall effect was softer and more pastoral, but I knew well enough that this was just a provisional impression caused by the season and the weather.

We were fast approaching the Sordkapp, the southern tip of Jan Mayen. I had never been in so close before. Here the mountains fell away to gentler contours reminiscent of the island's central section. Several tiny and perfectly shaped cones, perhaps the residue of secondary eruptions, provided the final oddity. The cape itself was a jagged staircase tumbling down to the sea. At its base a tall cave had been hollowed out, running right through the cliff; I could see daylight at the other side.

A little way offshore, rocks protruded, some tall and narrow, others little more than rough whalebacks. I wondered whether amongst them was the one which had done for Tilman's *Mischief*.

At ten in the evening, with the light and visibility closing in, we cleared the Sordkapp. Sixteen hours had passed since we had first tacked in towards the invisible base of Mount Beerenberg. The wind backed to the north and blew up harder. I reduced sail to a single panel and settled the self-steering to keep us heading slightly west of south. I cooked a hot meal and thawed myself out. From time to time I checked astern, searching for the fading outline of the Sordkapp. By four in the morning it was gone.

43

In one sense the voyage was over. My head and cameras and notebooks were stuffed full. I had seen as much as I could have hoped for. All that remained was to bring it all home across eight hundred miles of ocean, three hundred of them still within the Arctic Circle.

I thought about the long haul south, back to low pressure systems, back to shipping and oil rigs and land heavy with the concrete pustules and murderous charm of civilisation. In the course of just a few years I had spent over fourteen months at sea; intense, uncompromising months of trial and observation. I had broken through many barriers and discovered a view of the world that was refreshing and liberating. My vision had expanded. I had become a little wiser. The sea had taught me many unforeseen lessons but now, as we once again left Jan Mayen in our wake, I began to wonder whether I had reached the limit of what I was capable of harvesting. It was an unexpected thought, treacherous perhaps. There was no point in voyaging just for the sake of it, or simply out of habit; that was unthinkable. There had to be a sense of discovery.

Perhaps there was a sad irony here. Mount Beerenberg had taunted me through all my years of Arctic sailing, symbolising, perhaps, the unreachable, unknowable aspect of these northern wastes. Now that I had seen the mountain, did it mean that whatever need kept me going back had been satisfied? Had fulfilment extinguished desire? Was I destined to be caught in a no-man's land: sated with the sea and its wildness; repulsed by the excesses of terrestrial life?

I pushed aside this troubling prospect and concentrated on the management of *Mingming II*. There was serious work to be done, over and over, for the wind and sea state had combined to create the most unstable conditions of the voyage so far. The wind had backed to the north-west, and so we were running before it. It was a magnificently capricious wind, though, a typical Arctic wind, alternating thudding gusts with patches of near calm. It was impossible to find a weight of sail that suited both extremes. If I raised a panel or two we were overpowered in the gusts, griping to windward; if I reduced sail we wallowed in the calm patches. That may have been tolerable except that a heavy swell was coming in from the north-east and therefore nearly on our beam. With insufficient sail set the rolling was enough to cause a thumping gybe. In the right conditions we could run at perhaps fifteen degrees off square, but here I was forced to increase that to about thirty-five degrees to help maintain some stability. Even at that angle we were still gybing from time to time.

I was constantly at the hatch, adjusting the weight of sail to match the wind, changing the self-steering settings, undoing gybes and settling us back on our proper course. It was to be the theme of our passage all the way to the Shetlands, for the wind was to hold between north-west and north-east the whole way, with ever stronger gusts and lighter dead patches keeping me always at work.

Yes, the wind settled in from the north and gave us a rollicking run south and a string of daily distances of between eighty to nearly a hundred miles, but I earned every one of those miles. With the wind often gusting to Force 7 the seas built rapidly, adding to the instability of the ride. Over the years I had learned many tricks. The junk rig can sail happily by the lee, for example, and from time to time I could lock *Mingming II* into a firmer groove with the sail to windward and the self-steering and tiller settings adjusted accordingly. But nothing held for long. A cross sea or a squall or an over-violent roll upset the balance and brought the sail crashing across. In the strong wind I rarely had more than three panels set, and often just one or two, so the gybes were relatively soft. The constant repetition was wearing on the gear, though, and I was glad that I had built everything as strongly as I knew how. The additional anti-chafe protection I had put on the battens and boom and yard was earning its keep too: at the end of the voyage there was virtually no wear on the mast or spars despite the punishment they had taken.

In the constantly big sea there was less to look at, apart from the sea itself. Whales and their spouts were no more than fleeting glimpses, quickly gone. One afternoon we bore down on something orange. It was a buoyancy jacket and my heart jumped when I saw some movement in it. Surely I wasn't going to have to fish someone out of the sea? No, the jacket was attended by two fulmars pecking at the weed and barnacles that had grown on it. It was a typical ocean encounter: detritus that may have had a story to tell, or may have signified nothing at all.

At ten in the morning of Wednesday the twentieth of August we crossed the Arctic Circle. It was our forty-eighth day at sea, of which thirty-eight had been spent in the Arctic.

The previous night I was too hot under my blanket, and had stripped off my fisherman's sweater and track suit top.

The sky was still heavy with squally rain clouds, the wind still unremitting and capricious, so there was no end to the cycle of adjustment and readjustment. The sea was lengthening too, becoming more truly pelagic in its scale and rhythm. I sat in the hatch and watched the crests bearing down from astern; millions of tons of water in endless rotation, pushing us on and on. It was seductive, and mesmerising, this ceaseless motion. Light, sound, the sea; all formed of waves. Was the wave the fundamental expression of energy? Was there something in its geometry and movement that took us out of ourselves and into something more universal? Hour after hour I watched our rise and fall and listened to the hiss of the tumbling waves, hypnotised by their relentless undulation.

Sooty Shearwater

44

Later that afternoon, under a sky messy with rain squalls, two fishing boats blocked our path. They were trawling in random patterns, sometimes parallel with our course, sometimes angling across our track. Whichever way I turned we seemed to meet one coming our way. Finally I was forced to disconnect the self-steering gear and steer by hand, bearing away to the west-south-west, almost on a beam reach. It was exhilarating, for a while, to swoop and surf through the big seas, but this kind of roller-coaster ride was not really to my taste. I was forced on, though, with a pelagic fishing boat and its long trawl under my lee, until it turned and headed back east.

With the way ahead now clear we resumed our fretful passage south. The air was thick with spiralling fulmars, evidence of the fruitfulness of this part of the ocean. A check of my chart showed that this was almost exactly the spot where I had encountered a huge Russian trawler five years earlier. There was no obvious feature, such as a sea mount, to explain the evident richness of life hereabouts.

Day after day, the sky alternately cleared and filled again with overbearing squalls that blackened the air right down to the wave tops. I was at the hatch every few minutes adjusting and correcting. A brief flash of sun felt hot, and a gannet, the first sign of distant land to our south, cruised past on shallow wing beats. Next morning a puffin, and the only sooty shearwater of the voyage, reinforced the sense that we were transiting to southern waters.

My frustrated attempts to settle to a course continued. I sat in the hatch and considered the mechanics of the self-steering gear: wind vane turning pendulum; pendulum swinging and turning tiller; tiller turning rudder; rudder turning boat; and so on, round and round, on and on. I had watched this sinuous ballet for thousands of miles, fascinated by its power and simplicity. With a jolt I realised that something was not quite right. There was a sluggishness in the response of the servo-pendulum to the signals from the wind vane. Something was interfering with the usual fluid chain of command through the system. It was not particularly obvious, this slight inefficiency, but I ought to have noticed it before.

I immediately suspected what the problem was. I put on my harness, and armed with a set of Allen keys, exited the hatch and worked my way aft. Sure enough, there was the cause of all my ills: the servo-pendulum, normally vertical in the water, had pivoted on its bolt to an angle of forty-five degrees or so. At such an attitude it was almost totally ineffective.

It took no more than five minutes to fix, swinging the pendulum round and out of the water, straightening the blade and re-tightening its retaining bolt. This bolt is never over-tightened, as a precaution should the blade hit something solid.

I had skipped out on deck without bothering to put on my oilskins and sea boots, and inevitably paid the price. As we lay wallowing with the self-steering gear disconnected a solid green wave swept aboard, comprehensively soaking me. It was fair punishment for not having spotted the problem with the steering. I had little doubt that the blade had been working its way out of vertical alignment for a while, perhaps since Jan Mayen. Maybe it had hit something to start the process. It was almost certain, too, that it was the period of hand steering, when we had been surfing at relatively high speed down the wave faces, which had created enough pressure on the blade to push it right back.

Everything was now clear. Conditions had certainly been challenging even for a fully functional self-steering gear. For one that was partly disabled, they had been impossible. In effect *Mingming II* had been trying to steer herself downwind for perhaps a week or more. As I stripped off my sodden clothing I felt a pang of guilt: I had let her down. I was relieved too. With the self-steering gear repaired and working at full efficiency, our course was inevitably firmer and more settled. It was not *Mingming II* or her balance which had been at fault.

We passed 64°North. Massive banks of cloud poured in from the north-east, drowning us in torrential rain.

45

I had been at sea for fifty-one days: one thousand two hundred and twenty-two hours; seventy-three thousand four hundred and forty minutes; four million four hundred and six thousand and four hundred seconds. For every one of those four and a half million seconds I had been fully engaged with the boat and the sea, and with the concept and execution of the voyage. Even when I was asleep, a part of my subconscious had always been monitoring the sound and movement and underlying harmony of the boat. It had been fifty-one days of continuous application, with no distractions and no possibility of any distraction; nothing but boat, sea, sky and the creatures that made their home there. After four and a half million seconds of unmitigated engagement I was tired. The occasional undisciplined thought crept into my mind: how many days left? When might we arrive at Whitehills? I pushed these thoughts aside. There were only a few hundred miles left to sail, but those miles were quite capable of springing a whole new set of challenges on the enterprise. I knew well enough that I had to keep to the task, repeating the same simple and well-honed procedures over and over until there were no more miles to sail. There was no other way. The sea is a kind of prison, with no parole, no day release, no remission for good service. Every minute of one's time has to be served until the very last.

I thought more about this analogy. It was untypically negative, perhaps brought on by what was now a strong desire to complete the voyage efficiently and without mishap. For a voyage is also a kind of treasure hunt, and on this particular voyage I had amassed a whole sea chest of booty that I was anxious to bring home intact. Many of these treasures were evanescent, almost indefinable: a sudden view, a feeling, a moment of insight, a brief encounter. Nor were they treasures to be lugged home and secreted in iron-bound coffers. My task was to share and disseminate; to take these precious moments and reshape and reword them and send them out into the world as fresh and sparkling as I could make them.

The prison analogy fell down on another aspect, too. It suggested boredom, a forced lack of stimulation. I had long since learned that the continuous enjoyment of the sea comes from proliferating the categories and sub-categories of everything that one observes. If all a sailor sees is sea, sky, birds (usually categorised as 'sea-gulls', a gross and very lazy error), dolphins and so on, it is no surprise that boredom sets in. The interest is in the fine detail of every category, detail which, once one starts to examine it, can never be exhausted. Over there is a sea-bird. Very good, but is it a petrel, a tern, an auk, a gull, a skua? A skua. So is it a Great, Arctic, Long-tailed or Pomarine skua? An Arctic skua. So is it an adult or a juvenile? A juvenile. So is it first or second summer? How does its plumage compare with the young skua you saw yesterday? How is it behaving? Where is it heading? The questions proliferate. How are the other birds in the area reacting to it? How does its flight profile compare with that of an adult arctic skua? Where do they breed? And so on. This level of inquisitiveness can be applied to everything one is observing, inanimate as well as animate, until it becomes second nature.

By thus examining the minutiae, and recording it with notes, sketches and photographs, I had built a picture of whole swathes of ocean and the richness of its life. Patterns of habitat had gradually emerged. The most northerly petrel is the Leach's, but don't expect to see it within the Arctic Circle. White-beaked and Striped dolphins range as far north as Spitsbergen. Fin whales congregate to the north-west of Svalbard but not to the north-east.

I had become, too, a student of every nuance and subtlety of light, shape, colour and movement. Nothing was exempt from examination.

This constant search for every discernible detail of the pelagic world meant that boredom was impossible. I knew that I was privileged to be able to share this world for long periods of time; to have found it boring would have been a negation of that privilege, and a lamentable failure of imagination.

Thinking about it further, I wondered whether this passion for intense observation was simply a different kind of exploration. There is precious little left to explore, in the classical sense, on this planet. Satellite imagery has laid the world bare down to the smallest blade of grass. The lines are joined, the maps complete; at the cartographic scale there is nothing new to be learned. This being the case, had I instinctively recalibrated my exploration to the scale of a skua's tail feather, to the rippling of a cat's paw on a smooth sea, to the degree of coppering of an Arctic sky?

I wondered too whether I was engaged in an exploration of possibilities as much as an exploration of the physical world: the possibilities of one man and a tiny boat; the possibilities of adventure with minimal resources; the possibilities of integration with the oceanic world. Here were frontiers of a different kind still ripe for opening up. The world may now be an over-exposed global village, devoid of mystery, but for the fertile mind and the strong heart there are still un-trodden paths to be found.

North End of Uist from SE by E c. 15 miles

46

Sailing a straighter course, our daily run crept up to eighty-eight miles. Corrective calls to the hatch became less frequent, but there was still work to be done. After nearly two months of hard use the forward end of the top batten had worked its way out of its binding. The batten was retained by a line passed through holes drilled on each side, but there was no guarantee that the line would not fray and break. I donned full wet weather gear and exited the forward hatch to put on an extra lashing. While there I also reinforced the lashing of the sail's throat to the yard. There was something comforting about coming straight up through the coach roof to the source of the problem rather than having to work fore and aft along a narrow side deck. I was able to attach my harness to two strong points on the foredeck prior to climbing out of the hatch, and so always felt secure.

A ship crossed astern, heading south-west. We passed 62° North, running our way south along the Greenwich

Longitude. The rain squalls relented, leaving us to a trade wind sky and an easing north-easterly. I raised sail to four panels, checked the horizon ahead every few minutes and sure enough, at eight in the evening of Sunday, the twenty-fourth of August, our fifty-second day at sea, the hump of Unst's northern end, topped by a tiny pimple, pushed its way above the edge of the world fine on the starboard bow. Night fell and the loom of Muckle Flugga lighthouse cast a welcome glow. Other lights intervened, ahead and to starboard, probably fishing boats, and I resigned myself to a long and sleepless night. Throughout the hours of darkness the wind eased further, forcing us to six panels of sail as we threaded our way past the boats working in our path.

Just before five-thirty that morning I listened to the Shipping Forecast for the first time of the voyage. It may well be a heretical view in a sailing world obsessed with weather forecasting, but for an offshore sailor in a boat that averages slightly less than three knots, a weather forecast serves no positive purpose. After twenty thousand miles of sailing in the higher latitudes of the North Atlantic I had become so convinced of this view that I did not even bother equipping *Mingming II* with a barometer. What a liberation that had been, to simply sail and react to the conditions of the moment, with no care for the morrow!

The Shipping Forecast itself is delivered with such po-faced unctuousness that one would think that its words had been graven in stone and sent down from Heaven. Yes, it is a National Treasure; yes, it is Poetry and all that, but how often is at actually correct? Little more than half the time, in my experience, and if a forecast has almost as much chance as being wrong as right, wherein lies its utility? Structurally, it is a *reductio ad absurdum* of the intricacies and endless changeability of oceanic weather. Worse still, it creates unnecessary anxieties and unfulfilled hopes. It has caused me to stop when I need not have, and to race on when I ought not to. In any event, the concept of 'weather routeing', for a yacht that can cover no more than a hundred miles or so, on the best of days, is simply a delusion.

Nonetheless, with the navigational danger increasing in inverse proportion to our distance from land, it was now important to get some sort of picture of the general weather systems in operation, while retaining a healthy scepticism over the finer detail. In broad terms, the far north of Scotland was in for high pressure, with a severe low passing across southern Ireland and the south of England. That was as much as I needed to know. As far as the detail was concerned, we were promised easterlies, up to Force 5, which never came; south-west Ireland was due Force 10 winds, and probably got them.

By seven-thirty we were ghosting south under six and a half panels, fifteen miles to the east of Unst. A blue and rather ancient-looking oil rig supply ship passed close, heading north. We stuttered to a halt and I dropped the sail. Still not satisfied with the lashing on the forward end of the top batten, I made my way to the mast, on deck this time. With the spike of my rigging knife I gauged out two more holes in the batten and put on a second lashing.

The sky was by now almost cloudless, the wind gone entirely. For the first time I wedged open the forward and central hatches to give some ventilation. On an impulse I fired up my mobile telephone and found I was getting a signal. I rang Brenda to confirm my continuing presence on the planet, and Bertie Milne, the Whitehills harbourmaster, leaving a message to expect me within two or three days. By mid-afternoon that prognosis seemed unduly optimistic: since midday we had drifted south just over one and a half nautical miles. At that rate it would take us one hundred and seventeen and a half days to reach Whitehills.

The sea subsided to a mirrored calm and the sun beat down with what seemed like tropical intensity. From time to time the peace of the day was disrupted by the dyspeptic rumble of helicopters scything their way to and from the oil rigs. I sketched the hills of Unst, immobile to our west; curves interlocking under a single exemplary cloud. I thought again about the curious triptych of boatbuilding, navigation and writing, each dependent on and informing the other, their themes and motifs intertwined all the way through. I played around with numbers once more, and discovered that we had thus far sailed a distance in excess of a quarter of a billion inches, at a rate of fifty-four point one three inches per second. It was more than an idle game, this constant re-framing of time and distance. It served to undermine the comfortable norms that we take as universal truths. We have calibrated the world to suit our own narrow view; from time to time it is illuminating to consider temporal and geographic scale from the point of view of, say, a swimming crab, or an albatross, or a meteorite, or a mountain.

I listened to the early evening Shipping Forecast, which bore little resemblance to the one issued twelve hours previously. A faint insinuation of a northerly breeze scuffed up the surface of the sea, and with minimal expectation I once more hauled up all seven panels of *Mingming II*'s unlikely sail.

Blue Oil Rig Supply Ship

47

For five hours or so we faffed about, ghosting along hesitantly in downwind tacks. Towards midnight the remaining breath of wind swung from north, to west, to east, and then expired. I grieved for the dear departed, for we were left rolling horribly in a confused swell that had come up from nowhere. It was the worst of calms, the kind we had been spared for most of the voyage: a violent, crashing, infuriating calm. I lashed the rig down as tightly as I could and slept for an hour.

Just after one in the morning I spent a few minutes in the hatchway, checking that all was well with the world. We were now back to the darkness of real night, and the mast was girating madly. I heard a bang overhead, a nasty dull thud, and through the gloom saw the pale shape of a fulmar hit the water, wing first and heavily, a few yards to port.

I felt sick to the pit of my stomach. The fulmar had clearly hit the mast, or more precisely the mast had hit the fulmar. There was no question that the bird would die, probably by drowning. This was not something I could dismiss lightly. Fulmars had been our constant companions for years; that the reward for their curiosity and closeness should be an abrupt and violent death was an unbearable thought. I had always treated every form of oceanic life with as much respect as I could muster; I was, after all, no more than an uninvited guest in their world. My aim had always been integration, not annihilation. The death was accidental, but I was still its author.

I catalogued some of the unintentional murders of which we are all guilty, the ill-considered by-catch of everyday human activity: road-kill, creatures walked on, whales killed by ships' propellers, creatures killed by pesticides, vultures killed by veterinary drugs, albatrosses killed by long-lines, birds killed by power lines and wind turbines, animals and birds killed by humans' pets, turtles killed by ingesting plastic, wildlife killed by agricultural machinery, corals killed by acidification, birds and fish killed by oiling and pollution, and so on *ad nauseam*.

Every death was a negation of our humanity, a rejection of our true place in the world, a misuse of our intelligence. The thud of a mast hitting the light-boned body of an innocent bird neatly symbolised the schism that has opened up between man and the natural world. I heard the thud and felt in my guts the crumbling of bone and the churning nausea of our collective guilt.

I slept a short and troubled sleep. By four in the morning we were under way again; a firmer breeze had come in, again from the north. The wind held true, and strengthened a little more, and so there we were, rolling easily south under a brilliant sun, with the Shetlands laid out end to end to starboard. The only shadow on the day was the persistent image of a fulmar left dying in our wake. A yacht crossed ahead, heading east, the first sailing vessel we had seen for thirty-five days. My guess was that it was starting a passage from Lerwick to somewhere on the Norwegian coast. By mid-morning the island of Bressay was almost abeam, its seaward cliffs looking hewn and architectural. The soft slopes of the Shetland mainland behind, uniformly green, and topped with communications masts, seemed placidly pastoral compared to the excesses of rock and ice to which we had become accustomed. Here was order, and tameness; here, everything was subsumed to the commercial imperative. We worked slowly past Bressay, exposing the habitations sheltered behind in the approaches to Lerwick, and the red hull of a tanker anchored in the roads.

I realised why it was only the wild places that drew me on, why I had to keep the sea while voyaging: it was only the untouched that retained the essence of the world. The general overlay of human artefacts – houses, roads, harbours, cities, factories, malls, farms, refineries and so on – was a distorting mask; recent, provisional and in most cases uniformly ugly. Only in the open sea, and within sight of the pristine and the desolate, was it possible to penetrate the beauty and timelessness of things, to come a little closer to infinity.

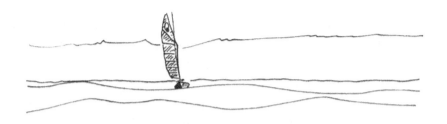

48

The wind held in the north, but once more fell away almost to nothing. With seven panels set I steered with the lines to keep us edging along on an acceptable course. We passed 60°North. Fair Isle, no more than a purple smudge, appeared on the starboard bow. The ebb tide held us up, the flood tide pushed us on, and a residual swell from the north lifted us bodily homewards every few seconds, but not without cost: every wave sucked the sail aft then crashed it forward. With more sea room in every direction I caught up on sleep in preparation for the final push to Whitehills.

The dominant point of reference was Sumburgh Head, the southern headland of the Shetland mainland. It had been in our sights for a day or two, first well ahead, then on the beam, and then astern. All the next morning it stuck resolutely above the horizon on our starboard quarter. It seemed to be sucking us backwards, or at least holding us by some invisible string. I knew that only when it was gone could my thoughts turn unequivocally to the last and most risk-prone stage of the voyage.

Just before midday the tide turned and the breeze swung round to the east, releasing me from the helm. With the flood tide under us we surged forward. Sumburgh Head disappeared.

Our noon position on Wednesday, the twenty-seventh of August, our fifty-fifth day at sea, put us just a hundred and twelve nautical miles from Whitehills. With the wind freshening from the east I allowed myself an optimistic calculation: thirty hours sailing, at an average of three point seven three knots, a not unreasonable expectation with a good beam wind, would bring us to Whitehills by six the following evening. It was a seductive thought: to be home and dry by nightfall the next day, without having to spend another night in increasingly cramped and crowded waters.

I am not normally a racer. I dislike rushing. I like to sail in a gentle and relaxed way, reducing to a minimum any wear and tear on both myself and the boat. The journey, after all, is the destination.

Here, though, the situation was a little different from the norm; it was a question of a safe arrival home after a long voyage, and of utilising ideal conditions to best advantage for the critical last few miles. I knew well enough how inhospitable the south coast of the Moray Firth could be. On my previous voyage in *Mingming* we had scraped in just a few hours before a ferocious Force 10 blow from the north-west, a storm which had rendered the whole coastline dangerous and its harbours inaccessible. I had my treasure to bring home, and here was a chance to do it quickly and in good order.

I made up my mind: for the next thirty hours I would drive *Mingming II* at full tilt. She would still be under self-steering, though, which meant the usual attention to balance; too much sail would overpower the Windpilot in the gusts.

Nonetheless I decided to push everything up a notch, to sail right at the edge of what was reasonable, and to sacrifice my usual comfortable progress in order to reach Whitehills, if at all possible, by the next evening.

With the wind ideally placed in the east-south-east and slowly strengthening, *Mingming II* bent to her task. Fair Isle was soon lost astern. By three in the afternoon we already had less than a hundred miles to cover. For the moment we were ahead of the required average speed, but there was no guarantee that this could be maintained for the remaining twenty-seven hours. The forecast was for strong south-easterlies, and so I allowed myself a sliver of hope.

On we raced, gradually reducing sail as the wind blew up more robustly. Night fell, leaving the eastern horizon aglow with the luminescence of a score of oil rigs. Ahead, almost on our track, lay the one possible difficulty: the Captain oil field. To keep to schedule we would have to past close by its western side. I could easily create a margin of safety by bearing off to leeward, but that risked bringing Whitehills further to windward. If the wind continued to veer, as forecast, the final run in could become a slow and difficult beat.

By one thirty in the morning we were down to two panels in a steepening sea. We were well into the gaping maw of the Moray Firth, a patch well known for its nasty conditions. For the first time in the voyage we were slamming, as *Mingming II* breasted each wave and pitched heavily into the next trough. On a normal day I would have reduced sail and ridden gently along, enjoying a pleasant nap or two as we went. Now I let her run on. In a way it seemed appropriate. This was, in all probability, the last night and the last muscular weather of the voyage. *Mingming II* had proven herself well beyond expectation. My confidence in her structure and her sea-keeping were now rock-solid. Why not give her a real test? Why not push her to the limits and see how she fares? It was a wild, bucking, noisy ride, and I enjoyed every minute of it. Once more the observation pod came into its own. I could not sleep, what with oil rigs just ahead, and support ships mooching around, but I could stay dry and warm inside. Sometimes the glare of the main Captain platform seemed to be dead ahead, and I was tempted to ease off, but I kept on, trusting that our ultimate course was true. Slowly the rig pulled onto our beam, just a couple of miles off, a huge unsleeping city, garish, alien, somehow frightening. A ship which seemed bigger than an oil rig rescue boat was patrolling ahead, back and forth, sometimes in our track. I watched without a break until it finally eased slowly to the east, leaving us room to pass in safety.

I hardened up a little, but not too much. The risk of being left to leeward of Whitehills had to be balanced by the need to sail the shortest course possible.

Dawn came and the Captain oil field was lost in the murk astern. The weather closed in, cutting visibility down to a mile or so. On we plunged, dancing a momentary *pas de deux* with an earnest fishing boat trawling across our bows.

By noon we had covered eighty-seven miles, and so were still on target for an early evening arrival. Three years earlier I had sketched the coastline and its wind turbines to help locate Whitehills from a good distance. That was of little use now: the thick moist-laden pall was unrelenting. The wind held, though, and so we careered in towards the unseen land, each mile making our hoped-for schedule more attainable. From time to time I tried to call up Bertie Milne, but the low cloud seemed to have deadened the signal too.

Our course still put us a little to windward of Whitehills and I eased off a little. The afternoon tide was now ebbing eastwards, so I was less concerned about being caught to leeward.

The coast was now just ten miles ahead. For a moment

the dark mass of Troup Head suggested itself though the mist before disappearing once more. Finally I picked up a signal and called Bertie, making a rendezvous just outside the harbour for six-thirty.

Now it was a race to be there on time. As we came into the lee of the coastal hills the wind eased. I raised sail but our speed fell away. Soon I had all seven panels set, pushing on a quickly as possible. The sea was smoothing, though, counterbalancing the falling breeze.

Even three miles off, the detail of the coastline was barely distinguishable; everything was blurred to graininess by the veil of heavy air. Further to the west the hills of Speyside stood out sharply under a brilliant sun. A large oil rig supply ship anchored off Macduff gave me something to steer by. I decided to pass a little to its west then bear away for the last two or three miles to Whitehills.

Using the forward hatch I looped a tow-rope around the mast and led it aft, its coil ready for use on the boom gallows. I put on my favourite Faroese fisherman's sweater, in honour of the occasion, and settled in to hand steer in the cockpit. As we passed the anchored ship and closed the coast the wind piped up again, sweeping across from the hills in rapid gusts.

What a joy it was, to sail in towards harbour with a fresh offshore breeze and a smooth sea! For the last hour we were back to sailing just for the sheer pleasure of it, for the feel of a yacht vibrating under the light touch of the tiller, for the rush and hiss of water creaming past the gunwale. Emptied of two months stores, *Mingming II* was at her best: light enough to race along with ease; heavy enough to feel secure and serene. She was looking better for the sea miles behind her: wind and sea had scoured her decks and coach roof clean and bright. I allowed myself a moment of boyish pride. Apart from some minor dislocation to one or two batten ends, she was returning home in as fine a state as she had left.

We rounded Knock Head and there was Bertie and his son-in-law's dory *Swee' Pea* making their way out of the harbour entrance. It was exactly six-thirty. The last half mile was now a beat to windward, but I didn't care. There was the harbour wall, there was the Whitehills church, there was the tight cluster of fishermen's cottages along Low Shore. Behind the village, and to the west, lay fields of golden stubble peppered with massive bales of straw.

I tacked in, making long boards to the west. Bertie came alongside. Aboard *Swee' Pea* was Graeme Gordon, who had helped tow us out, and Bertie's son-in-law Malcolm Jack. Also aboard, all smiles and blonde hair, were Bertie's two young granddaughters. It was not yet time to pass the tow-line. Bertie wanted to photograph; I wanted to sail right up to the harbour entrance.

For another fifteen minutes I played in the Whitehills approaches, working slowly in. The breeze was still fresh and lively as I put *Mingming II* through her final paces. We tacked back and forth, with *Mingming II* now under full sail, bending easily to the wind and slicing purposefully along. I could happily have sailed for another hour, enjoying this last moment of communion, but now there was no water left. I lowered the sail and surrendered the tow-rope.

Mingming II as I first found her in a sorry state. Perfect!

Building the observation pod.

Extending the cabin aft.

Most of the structural work complete for the after hatch and bridge deck.

Sewing the sail on the dining room table.

Carrying the lamp post mast from the house to the yard.

Mast stepped and hand-sewn mast boot in place.

On the way to her first launching.

Under sail on the River Crouch.
(Photo: Wendy Eagling)

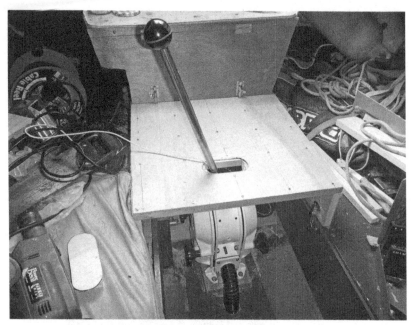

Fitting the big pump under the companionway.

Boom gallows fitted and leathered, and the solar panel and LED navigation lights in place.

The completed interior.

Mingming II leaving Whitehills on her maiden voyage.
(Photo: Bertie Milne)

Landfall at Bear Island.

Kapp Thor, Hopen's southern headland.

Humpback whale, with Kongsøya behind.

Sailing past the eastern end of Kongsøya.

We reach our most northerly latitude of the voyage, just to the east of Abeløya.

Temporary repair to the batten which had chewed through its pocket.

Mingming II's chart table, with galley under.

The working hatch viewed from below.

Approaching the northern end of the Stone Glacier, Edgeøya, in very poor light.

Kong Johans Glacier, Edgeøya.

The Stone Glacier stretches out astern.

Mount Beerenberg's crater shows through a gap in the clouds.

Closing the North Cape of Jan Mayen.

Making our approach to the Weyprecht Glacier.

As close as I dared sail to the Weyprecht Glacier.

Running down the west side of Jan Mayen, with Mount Beerenberg almost fully exposed.

*We approach the Moray coast, with Mingming II's Triple H TB
sail still working well after nearly 3500 miles of sailing.
(Photo: Bertie Milne)*

Arrival at Whitehills at the end of the voyage. (Photo: Bertie Milne)

Mingming II safely alongside at Whitehills.

APPENDIX ONE

Statistical analysis of voyage and comparison with *Mingming's* final Arctic voyage

Voyage	Mingming 2011	Mingming II 2014
Furthest point reached	80°North	79°North
Days at sea	65	55
Distance sailed*	3036 miles	3332 miles
Average daily run	43.1 miles	60 miles
Highest daily run	93 miles	97 miles
Lowest daily run	12 miles	13 miles
Total sail area changes	228	309
Average daily sail area changes	3.51	5.7
Maximum daily sail area changes	13	17
Total exits from hatch	20	17
Mandatory exits from hatch	10	13
Discretionary exits from hatch	10	4
Headsail set	4x	N/A
Wet weather gear worn	1x	2x

*   Total straight-line noon to noon distances. All distances in nautical miles.

APPENDIX TWO

MINGMING II – THE BARE FACTS

Under her remodelled exterior and new junk rig, *Mingming II* is a standard triple-keeled version of the Achilles 24. She is a derivation of the Oliver Lee designed half-decked racing keelboat, the Ajax 23. To create a cabin version, extra freeboard was added, increasing the overall length. The re-design was a joint effort between Lee and the long-time builder of the Achilles 24 fleet, Chris Butler. Fin and triple-keeled versions were produced. *Mingming II* is number 159 of about 600 built, and was moulded in 1980. Her principal dimensions are:

Length overall	23ft 9in
Length waterline	19ft 6in
Beam	7ft 1in
Draft	3ft 3in
Displacement	2600lbs
Ballast ratio	50%
Sail area	270sq. ft

The main sea-going renovations, modifications and additions are:

- Central keel dropped, sand-blasted, fibre-glassed, re-bedded
- Keel studs replaced
- Hull scraped back to gelcoat below waterline
- Topsides repainted

- Hull to deck joint strengthened with three layers fibre-glass
- New rudder and tiller built
- Rudder tube replaced with solid 25mm stainless steel bar
- New rudder stock
- Rudder shoe strengthened
- Rudder skeg refurbished
- New floors and cabin sole
- Whale gusher double-action bilge pump fitted
- Two watertight collision bulkheads forward, compartments foam filled
- Watertight bulkhead aft, compartment foam-filled
- Lazarette sealed
- Interior gutted and completely rebuilt
- Hull and cabin top insulated with 25mm Plastazote foam, carpet lined.
- New fore-hatch structure built to take Houdini hatch
- Long cabin windows removed, replaced with laminated ply and two small port-lights each side
- Dog-house/observation pod added with central Houdini hatch
- Cabin extended aft, to create working Lewmar hatch and bridge deck
- Cockpit lockers sealed
- Series drogue bins built on cockpit seats
- Stainless steel series drogue chain-plates fitted to each quarter with 3 x12mm bolts and backing plates
- Foredeck strengthened
- Mast step and deck partners built for new un-stayed mast
- Hardwood blocks glued and through-bolted with 12mm eyebolts each side of mast flange to take halyard and parrel turning blocks
- Mast made from municipal lamp post, finished with nine coats epoxy paint

- Stainless steel masthead fitting designed and built
- New sail sewn, with laminated pine yard and boom, carbon fibre battens
- Boom gallows built and fitted
- All deck fittings removed and holes filled, or where kept re-bedded
- Canvas mast boot hand sewn
- Spray hood hand sewn for working hatch on copper tubing frame.
- Origo single burner alcohol stove under lifting chart table
- Hellamarine LED navlights powered by solar panel.
- Various boxes built for shelving, with sailcloth covers
- Pulpit removed, rope lifelines taken from aft to midships
- 10mm U-bolts spaced along decks for double harness attachment

About the Author

Roger Taylor has been sailing small, engineless yachts to outlandish places for nearly fifty years. He is a recipient of the Ocean Cruising Club's Jester Medal, for 'an outstanding contribution to the art of single-handed ocean sailing', and the Royal Cruising Club's Medal for Seamanship, for 'exploits of legendary proportions'. He lives on a remote croft in north-west Scotland.